AGAINST ALL ODDS

The Donnie Hixon Story

Burt Reynolds' Stunt Double
in *The Longest Yard*

Stan Byrdy

ISBN 9781087815015

Printed in the United States of America
Library of Congress Control Number: 2019917684

For all general information contact Augusta 22, LLC at
againstallodds22.com

To the City of Augusta and
its many grand stories!

Thanks to the Byrdy family for their
loving support during this project
Donna, my loving wife
David & Hannah, our life
and Cotton, grrrr

-Stan Byrdy

To my beautiful wife Beverly
and my son Travis and his wife Allison
and to my grandchildren
Andrew, Katie, and Matthew

-Donnie Hixon

Contents

"...be prepared
to laugh
& cry..."

Inspiration

On the day he turned 75 years of age in 2016, Donnie Hixon, feeling a bit nostalgic, thumbed through the several photos that he owns of his older brother, Richard, and three photos taken in the 1940s of his father, Foster. The two died within a year and a half of each other when Donnie was just a boy. As he stared at the pictures, says Hixon, "a song was playing on the radio that caught my attention. It was an all-time favorite of mine called 'The First Time Ever I Saw Your Face,' and was sung by a favorite singer of mine, Roberta Flack. The single topped the Billboard charts in 1972 and help her garner a pair of Grammys.

1972 was Roberta Flack's year, and the next one was Donnie Hixon's — the one in which he was chosen by Paramount Pictures to appear as Burt Reynolds' stunt double in *The Longest Yard.* It proved a transformative two months for the famous actor and his acquaintance from Augusta. As Hixon became more comfortable around movie stars and football heroes that fall of 1973, he shared his story with Reynolds, and it was the budding movie great who first proposed that Donnie write his memoirs as a potential movie idea. One day, Hixon thought, he'd get around to it. Over four decades later from the time Burt originally proposed the idea to Hixon, that "one day" finally arrived.

With his gaze fixed on the old black and white snapshots on that milestone 75th birthday, a spark deep within Hixon was ignited and he felt moved to revisit the dark recesses of his childhood. Maybe not for a book, but at least a short story. "The next day," Hixon says, "I ordered the guitar sheet music of Roberta's song and played it as an instrumental on my guitar. Just before I sat down to write my story I would pick up my guitar and play the song..." Mesmerized by the tune, he couldn't escape the way it made him feel. But there was something else going on in Hixon's mind. While Flack's song was joyous, Hixon transfixed a polar opposite title to the melody and heard only "The *Last* Time Ever I Saw Their Faces" as the song played. Donnie Hixon began to write his memoirs "from the heart." It was Flack's song that proved the catalyst.

Over the next six months there were fits and starts with the writing sessions and Hixon says he "...started losing the confidence, motivation, and interest needed to continue, as it was too heartbreaking to re-live the past again." As fate would have it, a well-timed *AARP* magazine made its way to Hixon's mailbox. The publication's spring edition featured a smiling Sally Field on its cover. The connection to Burt Reynolds was immediate for Hixon, and gave him even more inspiration to keep writing. "...the smile on that beautiful face seemed like it was telling me to go back and write my story." Field and Flack double-teamed Donnie and the project moved forward.

Two years and 160,000 words later, Hixon completed his memoirs and provided this author, friend, and neighbor a copy. It moved me. I laughed and cried and began a rewrite. As a television sportscaster turned author, local stories of national interest have always been my passion. I transformed Donnie's memoirs into the manuscript enclosed in this book. Donnie Hixon's run-ins with James Brown, President John F. Kennedy, Burt Reynolds, Hollywood actors, and

NFL superstars are all part of his true to life, "Forrest Gump"-like tale. On February 1, 2018, Hixon and I made the trip 90 miles south of Augusta to the film site of *The Longest Yard,* Reidsville State Prison, unannounced — but that is a story in itself. Still, then-Warden Marty Allen made the prerequisite background checks and opened the prison to us! Nearly 45 years later, Hixon was back inside the prison walls. The memories from many years ago flooded back and I was there to capture it digitally. The pictures from the *The Longest Yard* were there, housed on the fifth floor, not far from the once operational electric chair, not far from the window that overlooked the one-time football field. Some seven months later, on September 6, 2018, Burt Reynolds passed away of a heart attack. Donnie Hixon, who had kept up with Burt through the years, and even visited him in Florida on occasion, was sad, but hardly taken aback by the news. "I'm sorry that he died," Hixon said, "but he had been in bad shape for many years..." Like the hard-charging running back Reynolds was in high school and college, despite his age and afflictions, he kept moving the ball forward until the very end. For the remaining months of 2018 and the first half of 2019, Hixon and I worked religiously to piece together this story. I poured my heart into the project and came to the conclusion that not only had I walked in Hixon's shoes, but from where I stood I could peer into his soul. Memoirs turned biography, *Against All Odds: The Donnie Hixon Story, Burt Reynolds' Stunt Double in The Longest Yard* is a passionate and powerful read, if nothing else, than for what Hixon terms "lessons learned." Grab a tissue — and be prepared to laugh and cry your ass off.

- ***Stan Byrdy***

"...the other
#22..."

Foreword

To hear Augusta, Georgia, native Donnie Hixon tell it, some of the best days of his life were the nine weeks he spent at Georgia's maximum security prison at Reidsville in the fall of 1973. It is also where he received numerous punishing blows to his body over the course of five weeks of intense scrimmages. After one such barrage early upon his arrival, a hit in which he was nearly knocked out, Hixon recalls thinking to himself, "What the hell am I doing here?" It was all part of filming for what became the classic sports movie of the era.

1974's *The Longest Yard* revolved around three players – Burt Reynolds and Donnie Hixon at quarterback – locking eyes with linebacker Ray Nitschke on the opposite side of the line. Being Burt's stunt double meant that it was Hixon who took the physically punishing shots from the likes of the fearsome Green Bay Packers Hall of Fame linebacker. Reynolds and Hixon both donned #22 jerseys in the film. The majority of live action scrimmage plays that were chosen in the movie were filmed the first three weeks with Hixon as his stand-in at quarterback. Reynolds ran some of the scripted plays.

"Let's make this clear," says Hixon, "he (Reynolds) didn't need me or anyone else to stand in for him. Had they let him, he would have been two times better! He was that good of an athlete." As noted in an article for the October, 2018. edition of *Columbia County, (GA) Magazine* written by this author, "Roughly the same height and weight, both (Reynolds and Hixon) were in tremendous shape, and looked enough alike with helmets on and slick film editing, that it was nearly impossible to differentiate between the two onscreen. Defensive players didn't care which #22 they tackled, they just wanted a shot at whichever *pretty boy* toted the football."

Injured playing football at Florida State, Burt Reynolds' dream of playing in the NFL came to a crushing halt. The top leading man of his day, Reynolds turned to acting only because he could no longer play football. And while he turned out to be pretty good at putting people in the seats, he'd rather it been as a running back, in a jam-packed football stadium. To earn a paycheck playing football with some of the greatest players of his era, for Burt Reynolds, *The Longest Yard* was a dream come true.

For Ray Nitschke, the recently retired NFL great, this was a chance to continue what he'd always done — play football. It also provided a cushion in his transition to a life without the sport, and gave him an opportunity to work out any pent-up aggression he might have in the process. That's where "the other #22," Donnie Hixon, comes in. Nitschke knew only one way to play — the full-out, Lombardi way — and he brought that intensity to the big screen. To this day, Hixon sports a mangled finger with a rod in it, courtesy of Nitschke, as a constant reminder of his days at Reidsville State Prison. Hixon's knee, the one he tweaked at Reidsville, was operated on several years after the film.

The Longest Yard also represented a dream come true for Donnie Hixon, "the other #22," who was denied the chance to play sports in high school. Hixon's is a redemptive tale that took him from homeless and heartbroken in Augusta, Georgia, to Hollywood, USA, as Burt Reynolds' stunt double in *The Longest Yard*. Maybe the greatest unknown athlete of the time, Donnie Hixon matched talents with the greatest actor of the era, Burt Reynolds, and Ray Nitschke, one of the NFL's greatest players of all-time. This is Donnie's story — *Against All Odds: The Donnie Hixon Story, Burt Reynolds' Stunt Double in The Longest Yard.*

"...young Burt was a scrapper, eager for mischief..."

#22 Burt Reynolds

Born at the family home in Lansing, Michigan, on February 11, 1936, Burton "Leon" Reynolds, was destined, it seems, to live life in the spotlight, in equal measures of times both good and bad. At the age of five, the Reynolds family moved to Fort Leonard Wood, Missouri, for two years, when his father was drafted into the Army. When his dad was sent packing to Europe in World War II, the family initially moved back to Lansing, then to Star City, a flyspeck of a town in north central Michigan where his mom was born, and where his grandparents owned a farm.

The Reynoldses took up residence in the small, family-owned cottage just across the road from his grandparents' house. A ghost town today, this tiny township in Missaukee County is where Burt roamed the surrounding woods and trails as a boy. For school, Reynolds rode the bus five miles each day to Merritt, an equally small community, which today lays claim to being one of Burt's childhood hometowns. Judgement call, but close enough.

According to Reynolds, in his 1994 autobiography, *My Life*, his mom would take him to the movie theatre once a month at Houghton Lake, some 15 miles east. The short road trip consisted of a five mile jog south along the unpaved Star City Road to Merritt, then east on M-55 for the final 10 miles of the journey. Aside from the Michigan woods and the movies, Reynolds' best friend was his radio, which got a new battery each month as well. High-tech for the times, radio brought the outside world to his isolated part of the world, where productions like *The G-Men,* and *The Shadow* came alive in his creative mind. Jack Benny provided humor, while journalists Edward R. Murrow and Quentin Reynolds, a war correspondent, kept the family informed of the world at large. Life was good.

In the spring of 1946, when Burt was 10 years old, and his father returned from the war, his parents went on a second honeymoon, and during their trip to Florida, Burt Sr., landed a job as a general contractor. Before the school year was out, Burt and his parents headed south to the oceanside town of Riviera Beach. His father, a grizzled Army veteran, had landed during the first wave at Normandy, and according to Burt, fought in the Battle of the Bulge and three more European war theaters. Burt Sr. was due for a reset in life, and sunny Florida proved just the ticket. At 6'3", 225 pounds, the imposing Burton Milo Reynolds later became police chief in the the tiny town on the outskirts of West Palm Beach.

According to Burt, in his autobiography, what he yearned for the most was his father's affection. But a simple pat on the back or an encouraging word were hard to come by. Young Burt was a scrapper, eager for mischief and just as quick to throw a punch if the occasion arose. Everything he did in life was for his father's affection, which seldom occurred.

Life on the ocean was worlds away from his years spent in Michigan, and changed again drastically for Reynolds some two years into the family's move south. Just as he was getting accustomed to his new environment, Reynolds was informed that his 7th grade class at Lake Park School was short on numbers. That necessitated him being bused to West Palm Beach's Central Junior High. The move proved highly unsettling for Reynolds in the short term, but altered his life dramatically as the script played out.

Compared to his old schools, Central Junior High was enormous in size and scope. Central shared its campus with Palm Beach High, the feeder school for 10 surrounding junior highs. Burt recalls, "... whole convoys of buses dropped off students, creating a scene that reminded me of the wartime invasions in Europe." Reynolds recounted in his autobiography that the "next six years of my life stretched out in front of me as if I had been drafted into the Foreign Legion."

In the middle of the chaos, Reynolds struck up a lifelong relationship with another student, Jimmy Hooks, who also didn't fit in with the popular kids, in part because he possessed a partial club foot. When Hooks reluctantly invited Burt to his friends house one day, they encountered his drunk mother and companion, and Burt witnessed the unthinkable. The man proceeded to push on his friend, and the scene escalated into an altercation between the two. Jimmy and Burt fled the scene, but not before his friend's shirt was in tatters.

The two boys walked to the Reynolds home, where Burt pleaded with his parents that Jimmy be allowed to stay with the family. As police chief, Burt, Sr. was likely already aware of the lad's plight. Reynolds' dad paid Hooks' mother a visit the next day to secure her approval of the arrangement. In 1972, the year prior to filming *The Longest Yard*, Burt's parents legally adopted Hooks, who went by the name, James Hooks Nicholson at the time. In his autobiography, Reynolds recounts stories from a younger age, and without mentioning him by name, simply refers to Jimmy as "my brother."

During his first two years at Central Junior High, Reynolds wrote in his autobiography that he was characterized as a "greaseball," or worse yet, a "mullet" from Riviera – *and that was just on the bus ride before he got to school.* Depending on one's status, students fit into one of a number of cliques at Beth's Soda Shop, the local hangout across the street from school. Being neither a jock nor a nerd, Reynolds ate lunch in the greasers' corner, while the popular kids with the letter-sweaters convened in their choice section of the shop. One of the best junior high athletes in the county, Peanut Howser, was part of the *in group.* You might know him better as former major league baseball legend Dick Howser, who managed the Kansas City Royals to the 1985 World Series Championship.

Though Reynolds wasn't an athlete, word got out among the soda shop crowd that he was somewhat fleet of foot, and Peanut called him out on it. Not that Howser would actually break a sweat in the matter, his was of the pedigree that initiated such challenges. Reynolds accepted Peanut's dare to match up against the school's fastest runner, Vernon "Flash" Rollison, in a true test of junior high prowess.

As Peanut and the soda shop elite assembled for entertainment, Flash laced up his track cleats and put his unbeaten record on the line. Determined to make the best of the one chance he might ever get to shake his bottom-feeder status, Reynolds lined up in bare feet, with heart pounding. David versus Goliath. Burt versus Flash. One reaches a bit deeper when the thought of being labeled "mullet" for life enters their psyche, and it was that way for Reynolds that fateful day.

With the urgency that one exerts when running for their life, Reynolds proved faster than a speeding bullet that morning, and showcased both his speed and dogged determination as he closed hard for the victory in the final yards of the race. In the time it had taken him to run the length of the football field, a mere tick of the clock in the course of a lifetime, Reynolds had morphed from wanna-be to real-life jock. It proved the breakthrough moment of his life, the one he would measure all his many career challenges and accomplishments against — a race he would continue to run until his final days.

Superman himself could not have flung the doors of opportunity open wider and the newfound confidence worked wonders on Reynolds. No longer confined to a telephone booth across the street, Reynolds would soon have new friends, a seat at the soda shop, and better yet, a nickname all his own. The future baseball great, Howser, congratulated Reynolds with a handshake and pat on the back for all to see, and muttered the words, "Nice race, Buddy." According to Reynolds, in his 1994 autobiography, "It was as close to a papal blessing as one could get." As for the nickname, "Buddy," it stuck.

And while he had never played sports, his new friend Peanut recognized the raw talent that Reynolds provided should he try out for football. Burt took him up on it and was selected to the county all-star team his first season. Not only could he run fast, but found he loved the contact. Burt added basketball, track and baseball letters that last year in junior high. Reynolds was living the dream he envisioned, all because he stepped outside his comfort zone and done the impossible — he had beaten Flash Rollison in a foot race. For the 14-year-old Burt Reynolds, the sky was suddenly the limit.

According to childhood friend, Wayne Elliott, in a *National Enquirer* article, circa 1979, Burt was just like the character he played in *Smokey and the Bandit.* He wasn't playing a part in the movie, he was playing himself. "He was a hell-raising, irreverent kid who had just about everything going for him. He was good-looking, the girls all swooned over him, and no matter how hard his old man got on his case, he couldn't give a damn." Elliott related, "His cocky attitude and misbehavior got him into a lot of fights." Burt's father taught him the same lesson that Donnie Hixon got from his dad in Augusta growing up, "Son, if you're gonna be in a fight, you hit first, and as hard as you can — and always be the one standing when it's over."

The future Hollywood stunt man, Reynolds actually got his start on that career path as a youngster. According to Elliott, "one of (Burt's) favorite stunts was waiting for a drawbridge to open, allowing the boat to pass, then running up the bridge as it began to close and diving 30 or 40 feet into the water. We all used to do it, but what made us mad was that Burt would cut it finer every time. He did everything for his own glory, but you had to admire his guts. It was a damned dangerous stunt. We could have been killed."

In that same article a girlfriend of Burt's in high school, stated, "He used to flirt all the time. I'd find out about him cheating on me, but he would always get around it. He was such a charmer and silver-tongued devil that you couldn't help but forgive him." Another childhood girlfriend was quoted in the article as having had a similar experience, "...another girl also had a crush on the good-looking youth, and it got to the point where Burt had both of us on a string. He'd see me one day and her the next." Yet another former classmate confided, "Buddy was so vain and conceited. Everything was stories about himself... He insisted the whole evening on being the center of attention. He didn't give a darn about anything except himself... He was so undignified. He just didn't have any class."

From the time he started playing football, the sport became his real passion in life, the one thing that gave him identity. At Palm Beach High, classmates simply knew him as "Buddy" Reynolds, the hard-nosed runningback on the Wildcats' football team. In his autobiography, Reynolds wrote, "Instead of cutting away from tackles when I ran the ball, I ran over them, and those I couldn't run over I punished for being in the way." In November, 1953, the *West Palm Beach Post* called Reynolds "the hardest running fullback in Florida prep circles..."

Still his father hardly noticed. In an interview with Marc Meyers for the Wall Street Journal in 2016, Reynolds related, "One day I had one of those great games and scored four touchdowns. When I came home my dad was sitting in the living room smoking his pipe. I asked him what he thought of the game. He said it was fine. I wanted to cry but didn't. I just went to bed. About an hour later, my dad came in. I'll never forget this: he sat down on my bed, put his hand on my knee and said, 'you were the best one out there.' Then he got up and left. I lived on that one rare moment for some time."

All-State and All-Southern honors followed and Reynolds was offered 14 college scholarships, which he narrowed down to Miami and Florida State University. Upon making his decision, the local newspaper announced his intentions to play college football close to home at the University of Miami. Again, it was Howser who challenged Reynolds to at least pay a visit to Florida State, where the Seminoles were upgrading their athletic programs to the major college ranks. After meeting with FSU head coach Tom Nugent, Reynolds signed with the Seminoles.

On September 18, 1954, in FSU's season opener, Burt Reynolds strode into Doak Campbell Stadium in Tallahassee for his college football debut, and hauled in a 33-yard pass reception in a 14-0 loss to the Georgia Bulldogs. Two weeks later, in a 47-6 win at Louisville, he caught two more passes for 36 yards and scored the first of two rushing touchdowns on the season. When the good folks of West Palm Beach opened their Sunday morning newspapers on October 3, 1954, they were greeted to the headlines: "Buddy Reynolds Scores in Seminoles 46-7 Win." On his early success as an 18-year-old freshman at FSU, Reynolds told the *West Palm Beach Post,* "I hustle, and I guess I'm lucky."

The performance earned Reynolds a starting role on both offense and defense in a 52-13 win at home over Villanova the following week, the only official starts in his career with the Seminoles. Reynolds showed off his defensive skills that day with a seven-yard pass interception.

Two weeks later, he showcased his speed and agility against Auburn at Cliff Hare Stadium, when he rushed for 62 yards on three carries, the bulk of it on one carry, which proved to be the longest run of his career. In his autobiography, Reynolds recounted the run up the middle, in which offensive lineman Al Makoweicki "opened a hole I could drive through, then I ran straight at the linebacker. Nobody did that. I duked him and then zip, it was off to the races." Literally. Fifty-nine yards later, Fob James, with world-class speed, brought Reynolds down inside the one-yard line, at the "one-inch line" according to Burt. Despite the run, the Seminoles did not score that day in a 33-0 loss that turned Auburn's season around.

After a 1-3 start, Auburn closed out the regular season with six wins in row that included four shutouts, then added a seventh game to the winning streak with a 33-13 Gator Bowl win against Baylor. As for the player who tackled Reynolds, Fob James earned All-American honors at halfback the following season, and later became Alabama's 48th governor, serving one term in that capacity, from 1995-1999.

Reynolds appeared in all of FSU's 10 regular season games in 1954, as well as the New Year's Day Sun Bowl. During the regular season, he tallied an 8.4 yard rushing average on 16 carries, and averaged 19 yards on four receptions. At Kidd Field in El Paso, Reynolds rushed seven more times for 35 yards in a 47-20 loss to Texas Western in the Sun Bowl. The Seminoles ended the 1954 campaign at 8-4 in Tom Nugent's second season as head coach. In the 11 games he took part as a freshman, including the Sun Bowl, Reynolds tallied 309 all-purpose yards the 33 times he touched the football — for an impressive 9.36 yards per touch. As he had been throughout his high school career, Buddy Reynolds was all the rave of West Palm Beach.

As good as the 1954 season had been, Reynolds' sophomore year was anything but as it spiraled from bad to worse, then out of control. Torn cartilage in his knee in September was followed by reconstructive surgery the following month. Reynolds quit the team without so much as a word to coach Nugent. Headlines in the *West Palm Beach Post* in September 1955 blared: "Buddy Reynolds Quits Seminoles Because of Injury." Still, he continued to put the Seminoles football program first over his own needs. He confided to the local newspaper that he would "feel like a leech" if he followed through on the three years that remained on his scholarship. Then came the holidays.

Feeling down on his luck over the prospect of never playing football again, the one thing that gave him identity, Reynolds borrowed his dad's '53 Buick for a spin about town. It was Christmas Eve, but Reynolds was not in a festive mood. Alone, he drove the evening away through West Palm Beach. As he headed home, his mind raced, and his car sped along too, at 105 mph — *more than double the 45 mph zone he traveled through.* The speeding ticket he received as an early Christmas present did nothing to soothe what ailed him. Nor did the circumstances that followed as he turned onto a dirt road off A1A in Riviera Beach.

In his autobiography, Reynolds relates that he saw the blinding headlights of another vehicle as he roared down the road towards a cement block factory. *What he didn't see* was the flatbed of the semi stretched across the road in front of him. In the split second from the moment he passed the vehicle's headlights, and glimpsed the impending reality ahead — Reynolds' ultra-tuned athletic reflexes took over and he dove under the dashboard. Good thing he did — his dad's car had just received a flat top — that is, the top of the car was severed from the body of the vehicle. Somehow the car continued on and rammed into a railroad embankment. As for Burt, he was held hostage in an entanglement of crushed steel and concrete blocks for *seven and a half-hours!*

In his own personal jailhouse, Reynolds was more worried about what his father, the police chief, was going to think. As the rescue team worked to free him from the wreckage, he recalled in his autobiography calling out to an officer from his dad's force who arrived at the scene. From deep inside the tomb of an entanglement, Reynolds pleaded, "Bib?... It's Buddy, Don't call my dad... Don't tell him about the car." To which the lieutenant looking down at the carnage replied, "I think he's going to find out anyway."

When Reynolds was finally extracted from the wreckage that Christmas morning, he stood of his own accord, without so much as a scratch. None of his rescuers could see the broken ribs, the mangled shoulder, or the re-injured knee that forced his exit from football. "I'm all right" he proclaimed. Strong-willed, world-class athletes have a way of pushing aside the pain and hiding the truth of their real medical conditions, from themselves, and others. Still, it was hard to ignore the blood that coursed from Reynolds' mouth when he coughed — that spelled trouble, and was something he couldn't hide.

An ambulance raced him to the hospital, and Reynolds' doctor from his high school days at Palm Beach High was called into action. Upon quick examination, Dr. Lynn Fort's instructions to a nurse nearby was of little comfort to Burt, who later distinctly recalled hearing the words, *"Prep him. This boy's dying."* They were not the words Reynolds hoped to hear. As his gurney traversed the hallway and the lights above flew by, Reynolds recalled that it all faded to black. During the operation that ensued, he also remembered hearing a nurse, *"We're losing him. I think he's gone,"* to which the doctor replied, *"Goddamnit."*

In what the *Post* reported as "an actual battle for his life," Reynolds lost his spleen in the operation that required nine pints of blood. Adding insult to injury, he also lost his FSU watch in the crash. When he awoke on Christmas Day, 59 carefully placed stitches along his midsection were there to greet him. Reynolds realized it for the miracle it was and that he "couldn't have wished for a better Christmas gift." A week later, on New Year's Day, Reynolds took a jog along the beach — a miracle indeed.

The head nurse in the hospital at the time of Burt's mishap later confirmed what he already suspected, that he had flat-lined that morning. Reynolds recounted in his book of "the whirling blast of light at the end of the corridor," to which he shouted, *"The hell with you, I'm going back."* The nurse told Reynolds it was then that Dr. Fort yelled, *"I know this kid, He's too damn tough to die,"* before he climbed over Burt and sunk his hand deep into Reynolds' chest, to massage his heart. The maneuver worked.

As the New Year brushed aside the past, Reynolds plotted another path forward. One door had closed, but a window of opportunity opened wide when he enrolled at Palm Beach Junior College and transitioned to acting. Cast in the lead role in the school play *Outward Bound* in April 1956, Reynolds was an instant hit. The performance earned him the Florida State Drama Award, and by June, he was on his way to Hyde Park, New York, on a scholarship for summer stock. There, Reynolds performed alongside Marlon Brando's sister, Jocelyn, in *Bus Stop* and Gloria Vanderbilt in *The Spa*, amongst other productions.

When 20th Century Fox witnessed his performance as Al in *Tea and Sympathy*, they signed Reynolds to a contract. The drama critic for the local newspaper was also impressed. "The standout performance in a supporting role was contributed by Buddy Reynolds. Perfectly cast as the athletic student, he looks like Marlon Brando, without the fishmonger's gestures or mumbling."

It gets better. By November, less than a year from the time of his near-fatal car crash in Florida, Reynolds debuted on Broadway, in the supporting role of Reber, in a revival of *Mr. Roberts*. The John Forsythe-directed production starred Charlton Heston as Roberts and Orson Bean as Ensign Pulver. Pinch me now, *but does this actually happen to anyone else in real life not named Burt Reynolds!*

Though FSU was squarely in his rearview mirror, it was never far from Reynolds' heart. Torn between an acting career and playing football, Reynolds headed back to Tallahassee in 1957. Nearly three years to the date of his freshman debut against the Georgia Bulldogs, Reynolds returned to the Seminoles backfield in the season opener against Furman. He carried twice on the day for 12 yards, and the following week against Boston College, returned a kickoff 17 yards. He did not take part in the 'Noles third game of the season at Villanova, but played defensive back in a mid-October home game against unbeaten and 13th-ranked N.C. State.

As the story played out, it was the 'Pack that sent Reynolds packing for Hollywood. In the time it takes a pendulum to fall from one side to the other, Buddy Reynolds' life swung from football star to actor. With just seconds remaining in a scoreless first half, NC State's All-American Dick Christy managed to get in back of two 'Noles defenders, including Reynolds, to score on a 46-yard pass reception — the only touchdown of the game. Burt maintained that Christy went out of bounds on the play, only to reemerge in back of the defenders for the catch, which would make him ineligible for the reception. That is, of course, if officials had seen it that way, which they did not. 'Noles head coach, Tom Nugent, saw it his way and laid the blame squarely on Reynolds' shoulders should FSU lose, which they did, 7-0. "The hell with it," Burt later recalled saying, and bid adieu to Tallahassee in favor of acting.

In the coming months and years, Reynolds transitioned from stage plays to television, then to the big screen. His first regular part in television came in the 1959 NBC series, *Riverboat*. Over the next dozen years, the one-time football hopeful fine-tuned his acting talents on *Gunsmoke*, *Hawk*, and the *Dan August* television series. But it was the 1972 film, *Deliverance*, that proved his breakout role in the movies, and established a path forward for Reynolds as a leading man. A series of box office sensations followed, including *The Longest Yard* (1974) and *Smokey and the Bandit* (1977).

Reynolds garnered numerous awards as an actor, director, writer, and producer. According to IMDb, the industry database that tracks all things film and television, Reynolds won a half-dozen People's Choice Awards among his many wins and nominations. He captured a Golden Globe for Best Performance by an Actor in a Television Series for his work in *Evening Shade* in 1992. In 98 episodes, Reynolds played the character of retired Pittsburgh Steeler Wood Newton, whose pro career was cut short by injury, a role to which he could easily relate. Newton returned home to Arkansas and a life he never envisioned, and Reynolds took it from there.

Reynolds saved maybe his best for *Evening Shade*, the creation of Linda Bloodworth-Thomason, who wrote the show based on the small town of Poplar Bluff, Missouri, where she grew up. A 1991 article for the Los Angeles Times related that when the creative writer/producer asked Burt what he'd have become if not for acting, Reynolds responded, "probably a football coach." Reynolds continued, "My brother (Jimmy) was a high school football coach for 20 years and when my dad talks about the two of us, he considers my brother as having a little more success than I have." Reynolds endeared himself to television audiences in the role as the captivating coach Newton, on a high school team infamous for their penchant to lose games.

Reynolds won a second Golden Globe and was nominated for an Oscar® for Best Actor in a Supporting Role for *Boogie Nights* (1997), a role he told late-night talk show host Conan O'Brien that he hated and turned down seven times. The film, about the porn industry, "just wasn't my kind of film... and made me very uncomfortable." Afterwards, Reynolds fired his agent.

But the biggest regret of Reynolds' career was a nude centerfold photo shoot for *Cosmopolitan* magazine in 1972, that came out just after *Deliverance* was released. Throughout his career, Reynolds lamented his decision to be photographed. "It was shocking at the time. It was meant to be, but I didn't know that it was going to cause a furor, and it did. If I had to do it over, I wouldn't pose. It doesn't get you work, for Christ's sake. And it makes a lot of men mad."

In his autobiography, *My Life*, Reynolds recounts that after the screening of *Deliverance*, British film critic Malcolm Muggeridge told him, "You're going to win an Academy Award." Years later, Alan Rifkin, who directed Burt in *The Last Movie Star* (2017), told *TooFab.com* the real reason Reynolds resented the *Cosmopolitan* shoot. "He felt that that lost him a nomination for the movie *Deliverance*... He felt people suddenly didn't take him seriously as an actor."

If *Cosmopolitan* was his biggest disappointment, playing quarterback in *The Longest Yard* (1974), was a dream come true for Reynolds. It gave him the opportunity to play football again and relive his glory days as a standout football player as a youth at West Palm Beach High, and in college at Florida State. In his autobiography, Reynolds related, "The movie itself was probably the most fun I ever had on a film, other than *Smokey and the Bandit,* because I got paid for playing football, which had been my dream since junior high school." Even better for Reynolds, he did not have to take the hits that his stand-in double, Donnie Hixon, endured. Hixon, from Augusta, Georgia, and Burt would become acquaintances during the production filmed in 1973 at Reidsville State Prison in Georgia.

In a 2017 interview for *Observer*, Reynolds made the correlation between playing high-profile sports and dealing with movie critics. "People don't understand the analogy of football and acting, but there's a great deal of it that's the same. You get dressed in the room and you think you've got it all prepared and later on in the game you wish you had put on more pads 'cause they're just kicking the hell out of you."

The media also reminded him of the roles he turned down, including Hans Solo in *Star Wars*. Reynolds told *Business Insider* in 2016, "I just didn't want to play that kind of role at the time. Now I regret it." He also brushed aside the roles of James Bond in 1969, Michael Corleone in *The Godfather* (1972), and as Garrett Breedlove in *Terms of Endearment* (1983), for which Jack Nicholson won an Oscar®. "I regret that one because it was a real acting part... it was a really stupid decision, but I made a lot of stupid decisions in that period."

In a telling interview with CNN, Reynolds confided, "I took the part that was the most fun... I didn't take the part that would be the most challenging."

Reynolds married twice, the first time to Judy Carne (1963-1965), and much later, to Loni Anderson (1988-1993). In between, Reynolds shared a five-year relationship with Sally Field, who starred with him in four films, including two popular *Smokey and the Bandit* productions. During an illustrious 60-year career that included numerous appearances on television and in the movies, Reynolds made millions of dollars, lost millions, and despite bad health, continued to work until the end. The hard-charging running back from West Palm Beach High and Florida State University, Reynolds continued to charge forward until the end. He earned a dozen film credits alone in the years between his 80th birthday in 2016 and his death on September 6, 2018.

#22 Donnie Hixon

Five years younger than Burt Reynolds, Donald Glenn "Donnie" Hixon was born March 21, 1941, at University Hospital in Augusta, Georgia. Donnie was the last of three children, all boys, born to Foster William and Dorothy Lundy Hixon. His mom, who went by the nickname "Treasure," was one of 10 children, and one of eight girls in her family. From the day Donnie arrived on earth that first day of spring, there were few "treasures" in his childhood and many more major challenges for he and his family to conquer. Burdened by a gambling addiction and a propensity to drink, the elder Hixon's vices combined to impose a crippling effect on the household financially. In an effort to manage expenses, his mother also worked.

Foster Hixon worked for a decade for the Fire Department, and then for a short stint at the Hill Food grocery store at the time of Donnie's birth. Fire Chief John Kennedy ran the powerful Cracker Party in town, and according to Donnie, it was the chief that helped his dad get the job with the fire department, and later had him fired. Then, to the family's elation, his father gained employment as a brakeman with the Georgia Railroad, again with the help of Kennedy. Stay on the good side of the fire chief and life could be pleasant.

When his dad was employed by the railroad, Donnie recalls that "He would ride in the red caboose... use his lantern to signal the engineer, and put red flares out to signal other trains... I have a very good picture of him... standing on the right hand side of engine number 326, wearing his bib overalls... (and) his cap, with his sunglasses resting on top of the bill." The cherished photograph is but one of the three Hixon family relics from those days. "I have never seen a family picture of all of us together, and no picture of me and my brothers with him (my father). Not even a picture of him and my mother together! You would think at least a wedding picture or some photo was taken of them together during the time they were married. Apparently we never owned or had access to a camera. *I would give anything if I had just one picture of him and me together...* Maybe someday I'll get over it! It hasn't happened yet..."

Donnie remembers that when his dad "wasn't working, sometimes you could find him at his main gambling hole at the Richmond Hotel in downtown Augusta on Broad Street, or at some other location that those in the gambling business selected and had set up. Per my mother, he sometime gambled away rent and grocery money by playing poker, blackjack with cards, or rolling dice. This happened often, and especially on, or right after paydays... gambling and prostitution during the Cracker Party days were widespread in the city and legal. A lot of families suffered because the working men in the family had this terrible, stupid habit. Addiction! Those running the show made money off the weak!"

Friends and Neighbors

At the time of Donnie's birth, the Hixons resided at 421 Walker Street in Augusta, in a house that the newborn would ultimately never live in. When his mom arrived at the location with her new son, one day earlier from the hospital than expected, she found belongings on the curb and was informed that the family had been evicted. Sympathetic neighbors took up a collection to provide the mother and infant with a Trailways bus ride to a relative's home in Milledgeville, Georgia. Donnie Hixon spent his first night "at home" some ninety miles away from his hometown of Augusta. Though it would be years before he could fully comprehend the gravity of the situation, the thought of what transpired that day had a lasting effect on him. "Sometimes that pill is hard to swallow whenever it crosses my mind," says Hixon, "and I have to remind myself that *what counts is not where you started out, but where you are today! Thanks be to God, I have been blessed!"* It was the first of many obstacles Hixon would be forced to endure in life.

When a repentant father made things right the following week, the family's follow-up residence was a wooden, tin-roofed house at 1838 Jenkins Street. The street runs parallel to Walton Way, the main tributary traverses from downtown to "the Hill" section, and in Hixon's words, "You might say this neighborhood was borderline middle America." Donnie recalls the Harrisburg section being "...a decent, old, established middle-class neighborhood for that time, with lots of trees up and down the street in front, and a lot of trees up and down the alley in back. Plenty to climb on... the street was not paved back then, but did have a cement walkway in front of some of the houses halfway down the block."

The family maintained the Jenkins Street residence until the summer prior to Donnie's starting first grade, one of 16 homes his parents rented during their marriage. They never owned an automobile, and relied instead on a bicycle, bus lines and "their own two feet." Hixon recalls that "The majority of families that lived in our neighborhood during that time didn't have cars either. Most of the families that lived on the Hill nearby did." If there were televisions to be found in Augusta those too would have rested on the Hill. "We never owned a television; instead, we listened to programs on the radio, and played 78 rpm records on our old record player, or played cards and checkers at night." By today's standard, the "good old days" of the late 1940s and early '50s were extremely low-tech. "We were down in the poor section down there," recalls a lifelong friend and former neighbor of the Hixons, Ernest Dinkins, who also attests, "We never locked our doors in that neighborhood."

Living under a tin roof that lacked insulation in the attic, when temperatures rose in the summer, not only could he feel the heat coming down from the ceiling, Donnie remembers that he could *smell* it too. "We only had a couple of small electric oscillating fans blowing hot air most of the time." Without air conditioning, swimming pools, or even a shower in the bathroom, summers in Augusta, Georgia, could be mighty uncomfortable. "It was nothing back then if you were playing outside or down the street and away from your house, that when you got thirsty, you would go stick your head under a neighbors outside water faucet to drink and cool off." The respite provided by a good shade tree during the day "or at night on the front porch when a nice breeze was blowing always helped." Friend Ernest Dinkins relates, "We opened up windows and put a box fan in them. That was our air conditioning."

The resourceful Hixon family and their neighbors also counted on other ways to beat the heat. "Sometimes we got to enjoy a good, cold piece of watermelon and cantaloupe," recalls Donnie, now in his late seventies. "Those, along with a big glass of iced tea or a cold drink, if you could afford them, were great thirst quenchers. All of these were great ways to cool down!" A bottle of Coca-Cola was 5 cents back then and "besides a cold drink in the summer," says Hixon, "you could buy a dill pickle packed in juice that came in a plastic package for only 5 cents. My favorite! I still see them in convenience stores today."

Friendships forged in the Harrisburg neighborhood growing up in the 1950s are among the ones cherished most by Hixon today. "My best friends in that neighborhood were Teddy Fulghum, who lived next door to us in the corner house, Ernest and Joe Dinkins, who resided two doors down, and Donnie and Harry Humphrey, who lived in back of the Dinkinses on Walton Way. Donnie Humphrey taught me how to catch pigeons. We got good at it!" It proved the happiest years in Donnie Hixon's young life. "I would never forget the friends I made in that neighborhood. Also, I would have good memories of the Easter egg hunts, the shooting of firecrackers during the holidays, and all the joy and excitement I shared with my family on Christmas day at that young age."

"Growing up in the South back then," he recalls, "all the kids stayed trim from playing outside in the heat, sometimes all day in the parks, school yards, other neighborhoods, and it was not unusual for us to return back home in time before the street lights came on. Kids were always playing outside! These were the days prior to fast food restaurants and you didn't see any obese kids. With no cell phones back then parents were not able to reach us during the day. The crime and dangers that exist today didn't back then. We played a lot of baseball, sweated a lot, and rode a bike if you were lucky enough to have one. We walked everywhere, ate mostly vegetables and fruit (bananas, oranges, apples, peaches, picked plums and figs off nearby trees) and we drank a lot of water."

Just blocks away, high atop the Hill on Walton Way, rested the landmark Bon Air Hotel. During the city's heyday, from the turn of the century through the Roaring Twenties, the edifice stood as a beacon for the rich and famous who wintered in Augusta. The "last stop on the railroad," Augusta, along with neighboring Aiken, South Carolina, 18 miles to the east, were the nation's premier winter resorts for those with money and status. Augusta proved a destination for Presidents, captains of industry, Major League Baseball spring training, and for a short time, the film industry. The great golfer Bobby Jones utilized the structure that overlooks Augusta as the unofficial headquarters for the Masters Tournament in its early years. The Hixon's eldest son, Richard, was born in 1934, the year the famous tournament began, and brother, Gerald, followed two years later.

While the schools the Hixon boys attended were located in the shadows of the grand hotel, the lifestyle it represented was worlds apart from the one they knew just blocks below. Those with money lived atop the Hill, and those without resided below. The income disparity between the two sections has grown even wider over the past three-quarters of a century, though the reach from below has encroached higher up the Hill. The aging Bon Air Hotel, one of the grandest structures in the city's history, today serves the Augusta community as low-income housing.

Richard, the oldest of the Hixon boys, was born with a clubfoot. "My parents had no money or any medical insurance back then to get any help." Enter Fire Chief John Kennedy to the rescue, again, along other local politicians, who, according to Donnie, "did do a good deed in getting Richard some help... he was finally accepted as a patient in the Shriner's Hospital in Greenville, South Carolina." Not only did Kennedy arrange for his brother's admittance to the hospital, "he personally drove Richard and my dad in his car, or provided transportation back and forth many times to the Shriner's Hospital." Donnie is especially thankful to Kennedy and the Shriners. "Without their help, (Richard) would have been a cripple for the rest of his life."

"...grew up in the 50s with attitude..."

Fighting for Foothold

Like Burt Reynolds and Ray Nitschke, two future American heroes who would one day cross paths with the youngster from Augusta in *The Longest Yard,* the trio grew up in the 50s with attitude, and learned to fight at an early age. Nitschke's father died when he was a child, Reynolds had a strained relationship with his dad, the police chief of Riviera, Florida, and Hixon's father simply wasn't around much. "When he came home like he was supposed to on a payday, hadn't lost any money, hadn't been drinking or gambling," Hixon related, "he was a great father, husband, and a lot of fun to be around, as told to me by my mom, relatives, and old friends of his. I always heard that in his younger days he was good in a street fight, and also in the boxing ring." The propensity to fight would carry over to Foster Hixon's youngest son.

When Donnie was a youngster, older boys in the neighborhood began to tease him about the onset of inclement weather, especially tornados, of which he had an overwhelming fear – one that bordered on obsession. He needed to be able to fight back. It was then that young Donnie got his first boxing lessons from his dad, who coached him in the basics. Hixon recalls as a five year old, "his outstretched hands, practicing a straight left jab followed by a right hand lead." Hixon was also taught at this tender age never to pick a fight, but if the occasion arose, to stand up for himself. The father ingrained in his son "...don't run, instead just walk up to them, aim at the nose, throw that right hand punch, and knock the hell out of them. That first punch is the one that counts!" The strategy worked, maybe too well for young Donnie Hixon. "At that early age I got into a few fights, punching them in the nose and whipping their butts for teasing me," Hixon says. "I bloodied some noses and busted some lips. After a few fights the word got out and the teasing stopped!

"I know it wasn't right," he continued, "but (my father) was right about the 'hammer and nail theory' he taught me. Always be the hammer and not the nail! My reputation as a fighter started way back then." Though he had natural tendencies as a pugilist, young Hixon was never a bully, but also not afraid to stand up for himself or a friend in need. "In those days," he recalls, "fights between individuals were very common, (fighting) one day and friends the next day." Characteristic of the times, film star Burt Reynolds, who would cross paths with Donnie Hixon more than a quarter century later, also recalled that his father implored the same advice. In his book, *My Life*, Reynolds wrote that "I can still hear my dad say, 'Son, if you're gonna be in a fight, you hit first, and as hard as you can — *and always be the one standing when it's over.*'"

Reynolds was quick to fight in Riviera Beach, Ray Nitschke was a brawler in Illinois, and Donnie Hixon stood his ground on the neighborhood turf in Augusta. When the three were united for the making of *The Longest Yard* movie production a quarter-century later, they likely represented the best actor of the era, the greatest football player of the day, and the toughest competitor the world never heard of. It was fate that the three "street" fighters would one day meet at a prison in south Georgia, still standing up to challenges.

Summer of '47

For Donnie Hixon, there were obstacles to scale at home growing up, wherever the family house might be. In the summer prior to Donnie's entering the first grade, the family moved to a sweltering cement block home off Milledgeville Road on Crepe Myrtle Drive. The hot-box of a home was located "out in the sticks" near Wilkinson Pond. This lifestyle was different from what young Donnie was used to. There were no neighborhoods with kids surrounding the cinder block home, or stores, or streetlights, or anything else that remotely resembled their home in the city. "The house was built on a cement floor," Donnie recalls, and "had two small bedrooms." Donnie, age 6, Gerald, 11, and Richard, then 13, all made room for each other and slept in the same bed.

The house, recalls Donnie, "had no city water or sewerage, only well water, and a septic tank in the back yard that had a slight smell to it sometime... With no shade trees, no air conditioner, and with only a couple of oscillating fans, it was very uncomfortable and miserable at times to say the least. We were there at the hottest time of the year in the middle of the summer, when in July, the temperature reached up to one hundred and sometimes over, and the humidity was unbearable..."

Living in that house back then, especially in July, was comparable to being in the steam room at the gyms and fitness centers today. Then at night, he remembers, "you had to deal with the mosquitoes if the open windows didn't have screens."

That summer of 1947, Donnie's dad worked for the railroad and like many youths his age, he was fascinated by trains. "In the back of the house was nothing but a large acreage of field and abandoned pastures... I would always listen and watch for the trains. Whenever I heard a train whistle in the distance approaching from far off, I would run as fast as I could up the field toward the tracks, to get as close as I could to the tracks, before the train got there. (Then) I would wait and wave at the freight train engineers in the front, and start counting the number of cars, (sometimes close to 100), and then wave at the railroad men riding in the red caboose at the rear of the train. This was very exciting, and I would run back home and tell my mom the railroad men saw me and waved. I also would tell her how many cars I counted. We also used to go out on a clear night," says Donnie, "and my brothers taught me to identify the locations of the North Star and the Little and Big Dippers." Donnie and his brothers made the best of life outside of the city.

Another positive about living out in the sticks, remembers Donnie, "was being able to go to Wilkinson's Public Swimming Pond which was about a quarter of a mile up Milledgeville Road from us. We would dam up nearby Rocky Creek to cool off and occasionally slip in a watermelon to chill overnight. My brothers and I would walk out of the neighborhood... with our bathing suits or shorts on, and go swimming there whenever we had the money. We didn't have to carry any towels to dry off after we were through swimming, because that summer heat would get you dry quick... My brothers were excellent swimmers and taught me how to dog paddle before they threw me into the roped-off eight-foot deep section where I learned to swim, and gained confidence in the water. Thus, I was not scared to jump off the diving board, and go down the slide by myself. I got to give my brothers credit, they were very good teachers. As they say in today's world, 'I knew that they had my back!'"

The simple things in life many times bring back the fondest memories, as Hixon attests, "We would walk back alongside Milledgeville Road in the tall grass, and weeds to avoid walking on the hot pavement. I remember when it got time to cross the road, we would race, running as fast as we could crossing the hot pavement in our bare feet." Those moments "are very special to me," Donnie reminisces, "because all three of us (my brothers and I) were around each other all the time during that summer, doing everything together. Great memories!"

The slow pace of living outside the city, however, would not be without peril. Donnie remembers one frightful day that summer when his dad was away from home with the railroad, and his brothers were off swimming at Wilkinson's Pond. The house to the one side of their house was rented by a young soldier from Fort Gordon and his wife. "The house to the right of ours was occupied by a family that included a middle-aged man named Sloan. Even today I remember him and that name! He was a member of the family that owned the property. You might say he was the black sheep of the family."

Alone at home with his mom,"Sloan saw us outside and kept staring at us, and slowly started to stagger toward us," Donnie recalls. "He apparently had been drinking heavily and started cursing and shouting at my mom, saying he was coming over to see us and collect the rent one way or another. Sometimes he would collect the rent," says Donnie. "He probably had other intentions on his mind. My mom grabbed me, took us into the house, shut the front door, and tried her best to keep him from getting inside."

The determined Sloan, remembers Donnie, "was beating on the door, screaming for her to let him in, and hollered that if she didn't, he was going to teach her a lesson." All the commotion and screaming drew the attention of the soldier to the other side of us, who had just got home from work. He saw what was going down, and immediately went inside and called the police. I was crying and my mom was yelling and screaming at Sloan to go away and leave us alone. But he being the stronger, won the battle and overpowered mom and got the door open, then tripped and stumbled to the floor."

Donnie recalls, "We then ran to the bedroom and mom pushed the dresser and the bed in front of the door, and we ran to the window screaming and hollering for help. We could hear the drunken man banging, stumbling, and falling against the door trying to get up. That old window was stuck and wouldn't open... high enough so we would be able to could crawl out... I was scared and shaking all over. Just in the nick of time, my brothers, on their return home heard us screaming and came running in, just as the police arrived. Before the police got in, my older brother Richard, who would become the baseball player in the family had grabbed the baseball bat that was against the living room wall, and laid Mr. Sloan out." When his brother tattooed the man's back with the Louisville Slugger®, a .45 caliber military pistol fell to the floor. The gun was confiscated and the assailant led away in handcuffs. "The police said Richard was very brave and a hero for his quick actions that saved us from harm."

"Before (the police) left they told mother not to worry as he would be locked up for a while, and advised her it would be in our best interest to move out of there... Dad had already been looking to get us out of that place and found us a better place..." Just shy of three months at the cement house, and hardly quick enough, the Hixons moved back to the city, three blocks from their former Jenkins Street residence.

The house at 1013 Holden Street was across the main thoroughfare, Walton Way, and close enough that Donnie was reunited with friends from his old neighborhood. The family moved into their new surroundings just a week prior to Donnie starting first grade.

“...I bit the shit out of him...”

Armed to the Teeth

At a young age, Donnie Hixon had a propensity to leave his mark — his teeth marks — on more than one individual. He recalled, "...my brother Gerald loved to sit on the porch during a rain storm to watch the lightning and hear the thunder. He was never scared of thunderstorms. Once during a storm he tried to get me to sit on the front porch with him. Being five years older and stronger, he grabbed me up and carried me, screaming and fighting, out of the house. I fought hard as he tried to hold me down on the porch while the lightning storm was going on. After I bit the daylights out of him, he quickly turned me loose, and I ran back in the house and hid. He gave up on that idea and never tried that again. He was only trying to help, and he thought this would help me to not be afraid of storms. It didn't work. If a storm happened at night I hopped in the bed between dad and mom and hid under the covers."

The first day of grade school for Hixon, like many children his age, also proved a bit unnerving, in part, Donnie says, "because I hadn't taken part in preschool, social, or church group activities prior to the start of formal education." When the shy youngster was finally coaxed to take his turn at the front of the classroom and introduce himself to classmates at Joseph Lamar Elementary School, some in the audience began to laugh. "If you think they were laughing then," recalls Hixon, "they really got loud when *I jumped out the nearest big window.* We were on the first floor, and not that high off the ground. When I landed, I was off and running, and as I looked back, they were all looking out the windows and laughing at me as I ran across the school yard, headed for home (three blocks away), and hid. *Can you believe it, I didn't make it the first day!"*

When Hixon arrived for school with his mother a half-hour early for the second day of school, the principal tried to get him to talk about the previous day's misadventure. "Hardheaded me would not answer, cooperate, or talk to him," says Hixon. "I just kept crying. I was a stubborn little brat! Finally the principal made the decision that I had to be punished, and he got mom's permission to paddle me. That still didn't scare me. He made a big mistake when he grabbed hold of me trying to get me across his lap. I gave him a rough time fighting back, screaming and hollering, and determined not to let him paddle me, but he being an adult, and a lot stronger, he won out. Finally he got me across his lap and *I bit the shit out of him* on his left thigh... He was still hollering when I ran out the front door of the school. *I have now missed the first two days of school!"* If only the ongoing saga of Hixon's first days in school ended there.

"The next morning my mother had my brother Gerald, a 6th grader at the school, take me to the classroom. Before I even got a chance to sit down, some of the students... started laughing while pointing at my pants. The last thing Hixon remembers, "I heard Ben Cheek, a longtime best friend, holler out, 'there he goes again' as *I jumped out the window again. Now I've missed the first three days of school.* My brother said the teacher told him I was really getting good at jumping out that window!"

Upon further investigation, his brother was able to determine that Donnie's problem stemmed from "knickers" that his Aunt Sara from Macon, Georgia, purchased at a bargain price. "Golfers in Great Britain wore them in the day," Hixon attests. Even for a poor kid who grew up in the shadow of the Masters Tournament, whose patron saint Bobby Jones sported the attire throughout the 1920's — by the mid-40's, plus-fours had well run their course. "They were ridiculous and funny looking to say the least, especially when I was the only one in school with those kind of outdated pants on. It might have been funny to them, but not to me!" When his mother purchased blue jeans (short pants were not allowed in the day at school) for her son, the episodes finally stopped. "I didn't get laughed at anymore, made it the whole day, and couldn't wait to go back to school the next day!"

"...ran fast
as I could
to see him..."

The Last Time Ever I Saw His Face

Fast forward two years to Thursday, October 20, 1949, a day that began like any other in the Hixon household. Donnie was in the third grade when he got home from school that autumn afternoon. His brother, Gerald, then an eighth grader, was at football practice at nearby Tubman Middle School on Walton Way, and the family's oldest sibling, Richard, was off on his bicycle, collecting on his newspaper route. Donnie's mom arrived home shortly afterwards and the two awaited the arrival of his father, who had spent the previous two nights away from home with his job on the railroad. The bus stop was situated just two blocks away at the main thoroughfare, Walton Way. "After a while as I was sitting on the porch I heard him whistling and coming up the sidewalk," Hixon recalls, "wearing bib overalls, and with sunglasses on the bill of his railroad cap. I jumped off the porch all excited and ran fast as I could to see him. He was carrying his lunch box in one hand, grabbed me with the other and threw me over his shoulder as he walked toward the house." If he could freeze-frame one moment in time, for Donnie Hixon, *it would be that one.*

Shortly after the father and son entered the house, his parents began to quarrel and Donnie was sent outside. Donnie suspects that his highly jealous father may have confronted his wife about a ride home from work she accepted from another man. The topic quickly escalated to a bad check written by his father and his drinking habit. The eight-year-old related that he heard things a child should never hear — cursing and threats and the next thing he knew, "one cop pulled up in front of the house in a patrol car, followed by two motorcycle cops, and another cop driving a paddy wagon." Foster Hixon was already on the police department's radar regarding a parole violation for writing bad checks, and coupled with the domestic dispute, warranted the response of additional officers.

"One of them hollered at me to go tell my dad to come outside," recalls Hixon. When his enraged father emerged from the house, he was summoned by a policeman at the bottom of the steps, to *"Get down here!"* His father leapt down the steps with fists flying, and according to Hixon, the policeman sustained a bloody nose and face, then fell backward to the ground. The other three policemen joined the fray, including one with a blackjack, and the group eventually pummeled Hixon's father to the ground, but not before Foster Hixon sustained severe blows to his head and face. The struggle continued even as his father was on the ground and the police continued to pound and kick his father with blows as they attempted to secure him with handcuffs. The officer with the handcuffs had one knee on the ground and the other extended behind himself.

That's when eight-year-old Donnie moved into action. "I only weighed probably 45 pounds and tried to help my dad. Scared they might hurt me, my mom kept hollering, "Get back on the porch Donnie!" Despite his moms instructions otherwise, Donnie continued on and wrapped his arms around one of the policeman's ankles. "The officer's pant leg had gotten pulled up in the scuffle," Hixon recalls, "and I sunk my teeth real good into his skinny-assed calf," just above his ankle.

For the second time in a year, with the school principal being his first victim, Hixon left his teeth marks on another human being. Years later Hixon's mom told Donnie the officer was screaming for someone to get him off his leg. "Another policeman jerked me by the legs and threw me on top of the hedges on the side of the yard.

"I remember my mother shouting at the policemen as they carried dad handcuffed to the paddy wagon, who were still hitting and kicking at my father. 'He's had enough, please quit,' she yelled, 'you're going to kill him!'" In looking back, Hixon maintained, "He was lucky they didn't shoot him. In today's world they likely would have." In his heart today, Hixon maintains, "I still will always believe if my older brother Richard, who was collecting his paper route, had been home that afternoon dad would have not acted abusive or talked to my mom that way in front of him, and it wouldn't have been necessary for mom to call the police. We will never know."

What happened next is ingrained in Hixon's memory. The officers threw his father in the paddy wagon, and afterwards, Hixon remembers that the policemen chuckled and reveled in their victory. He recalls that his father leaned against the bars at the back of the wagon, and with his bloody face peered out at his young son. "The wagon pulled off slowly along the dirt road and jerked my dad back down. I ran as fast as I could trying to keep up with that paddy wagon, crying out for my dad... in the cloud of dust it whipped up as it rolled along." Meanwhile, his father had gotten back up and, Hixon recalls, "I could see his hands gripping the small window bars, holding on to look out at me... at eight years old, what a terrible experience this was for me to witness, one I've never forgotten."

The next thing Donnie remembers is that "I stumbled and hit the ground, skinning my knees, hands, and elbows and ended up laying on my stomach, as I watched that paddy wagon travel on down the street, stopping at Walton Way, make a right turn and disappear. While she was putting iodine on the scrapes I received from the fall on that dusty gravel road, I told my mom, 'Don't worry; when I grow up I'm going to get them back.' That really upset her, and she said, 'You don't talk that way, or you will be making the same mistake your dad did.' I promised her I wouldn't try to fight four of them — instead, I would get them one at a time. *I did get that chance 10 years later!* Up until the time I went in the Marines, I didn't care much for policemen." Hixon recognizes today that most policemen are good, law-abiding citizens. "But some police in those days had a bad reputation for being bullies, hiding behind their badges and beating up on drunks and innocent people when it wasn't necessary... they could get away with it!" Hixon says.

It would take a stint in the Marines for Hixon to soften his heart toward the men in uniform, and through the years, Hixon has gained great wisdom. "The lesson I learned from this," says Hixon, "is to cooperate with the police if you get caught breaking the law. My dad made a stupid decision and bad choice that ended up costing his life... It is very sad because it is the families of the victims who are the ones who get hurt the worst. This I do know firsthand. It breaks my heart to see this happen... and it takes me back in time to that fall afternoon of Thursday, October 20, 1949... (that) left me and my brothers without a dad. It all started with him, and the situation could have, should have, and would have been avoided had my brothers been there."

When Donnie's two brothers came home that evening, they were informed of the happenings. After supper, the saddened family sat and wondered aloud about their father. Upset and afraid, young Donnie found it hard to sleep that night, and crawled into bed with his mother. Around 3 o'clock in the morning of Friday, October 21,

1949, Hixon heard the patrol car as it pulled up in front of the house. Moments later an officer knocked on the door and asked Donnie to get his mother. "I can still see my mom tying the ropes on her robe as she walked to the front door." The officer instructed her to follow along to their neighbor's house, who the Hixons knew best, while his mom repeatedly asked, *"What is this all about?"* Donnie followed along quickly in their footsteps to the neighbor's house, where the officer rang the door bell and knocked until finally the lights came on at that early morning hour. The officer requested to enter the house with Donnie's mother, and instructed Donnie to remain on the porch.

The young boy ran to an open window on the porch, pressed his ear close to the screen and heard the officer tell his mother, "I've got bad news, your husband is dead." The eight-year-old Hixon remembers how his mother screamed at the officer and requested to know how her husband died. As the young boy listened intently, he recalled the officer's response. "He hung himself in the jail!" At that, Hixon recalls that his mother "started screaming, slapping, and shouting at (the officer)." Hixon's mother insisted that her husband "didn't kill himself, that they (the police) beat him to death." As Hixon's neighbors restrained his mother, Hixon recalls that he also was in a state of shock and rage. "...full of fear and anger I ran into the street crying. I was going to retaliate and get even with that policeman, so I picked up some rocks and started throwing them at him, hitting him in the leg with one as he was walking back to the car."

A neighbor across the street, stirred from their sleep by the commotion, years later told the young boy that he heard the policeman attest, "I'm not the one who beat up on your daddy, son." With that, the officer returned to his patrol car. "No one back then ever believed my dad hung himself in jail," said Hixon. "That look I saw on his face as I was falling to the ground (behind the paddy wagon the previous day) turned out to be *the last time I would ever see his face... alive."* The account in *The Augusta Chronicle* of October 21, 1949, read "Man Hangs Self In Police Lockup." The newspaper reported that Hixon's father was found by a "cell block officer, at five minutes after one, hanging by his belt... He was cut down immediately and and was rushed to the hospital but was lifeless on arrival at the infirmary." Donnie Hixon calls the newspaper account into question. Hixon's father was wearing bib overalls that night as he always did for his job at the railroad. He was was not wearing a belt that night. "What efforts were in place to try and revive him," Hixon asks.

Before the young boy could process all that had transpired, funeral services were held for his father that very Saturday, October 21, 1949, less than 48 hours from the time his dad returned home from work. It would be the first time the eight-year-old Donnie was ever inside a funeral home. He had heard talk from his uncles and others that despite the cosmetic endeavors the undertaker performed with make-up, one could still see that his father had taken "a terrible beating." Then came the moment Donnie dreaded most — when he would see his father for the last time. "I was crying my heart out," Hixon recalls, "really scared, and was very nervous about seeing him. One of my uncles took me in the room where dad was and said, 'You got to tell your dad goodbye, he would want you to!' He picked me up and held me up over the casket and just above my dad's face. I looked down into his face knowing that I would never see him again, and with all my courage, strength and whatever I had left in me, I said, *'Goodbye, I love you Dad, I don't want you to go!'* I started screaming and was continuing to cry my heart out as my uncle sat me back down on the floor. I noticed everyone in that room around me had started crying again. I will never forget looking at him for that last time! *This was the last time I ever saw his face!* He was dead and I would never get to see my dad again!" Even as a young boy, Donnie Hixon knew "The damage was done. Our lives would never be the same... mine wouldn't. My dad was not going to be a part of my or my brothers' lives ever again! I was going to grow up without a dad!"

"When we arrived at Westover Cemetery on the Hill," Hixon remembers, "I watched as they unloaded his casket, carried it, and set it over the six-foot hole next to the road side. The family was being seated under the tent that was set up with chairs, and the preacher did some more talking and the crying started all over again, and even more afterwards when you heard the chains lowering the casket. That noise put chills all through my body. I remember being so scared, crying and shaking all over, watching that casket go into the ground, seeing my dad being buried! While the casket was being lowered the preacher was saying the 23rd Psalm. After that it was all over. He was gone."

Bright and early Monday morning, Hixon was back in school — because that's what you did in those days. There was no counseling available for either Hixon or his schoolmates. "I remember seeing classmates and the teachers looking real sad while they were staring at me most of the day. It was as if they were scared of me and didn't have much to do with me, and for what reason I didn't know. Later on some got a little brave... and asked me, *'Did your dad really hang himself? That hurt!'"* There was a stigma attached to suicide and according to Hixon, in the late 1940s and early '50s people oftentimes distanced themselves from families that had experienced such a tragedy, feeling that another member of the same family might be susceptible. From that point on, Hixon felt ostracized, shunned at an early age for something outside his control — something to this day he doesn't believe was even true.

Over the years, Hixon heard other stories in connection with his father's death. In one such account, an Augusta policeman years later told his wife "that my dad did not hang himself." According to Hixon,

"He (the officer) didn't, or for some reason wouldn't, tell her how (Hixon's father) died, only that he didn't hang himself..." According to Hixon, "...the jailer, making his rounds, found (his dad) lying on the floor and he had died from head injuries, and that the police made a mistake by not taking him to the hospital for treatment. Some say when they were getting him out of the paddy wagon, (his father and the officers) had words, and they beat on him some more!" Hixon also recalled another such story in which, "One person who was in jail at the time, said later he saw (policemen) carrying (his dad) to his cell..." Hixon surmised that "This could have meant he was unconscious or was already dead."

With the aid of additional research by this author, Hixon read archives from the local newspaper account of those fateful days for the first time in May 2019. The front page of *The Augusta Chronicle* on October 21, 1949, reported the story on the first column, just under the fold. In small, bold type, the heading read, "Man Hangs Self In Police Lockup." The writeup continued that Foster Hixon "was found by H. C. Deas,, cell blocks officer, at five minutes after one o'clock hanging by his belt..."

Seven decades later, Hixon maintains that the report carried in the *Chronicle* was not an accurate account of what happened that evening. First, his father "was wearing bib overalls, and no belt." Hixon asks, "Where did the belt come from?" Second, the account did not mention "the terrible beating (his father) took at the hands of the police." Finally, according to the newspaper report "there was plenty of body heat when he (Foster Hixon) was placed in the ambulance." Donnie asserts that "there was no mention of CPR attempted by Officer H. C. Deas. Police today know CPR, but I don't know that they did back then." According to Hixon, the "police would have had a tough time explaining how he died from the beating he received, and instead said he hung himself." Hixon believes his father died of cerebral hemorrhage the result of the beating he and his mother witnessed at the hands of police that night.

Hixon asserts, "These coverups happened to a lot of people back in the day. What really was the cause of my dad's death? There was talk around town it was because of the beating he took." Many years have come and gone since the day Donnie's father died, but the scars from that autumn day in 1949 remain fresh in Hixon's mind. "Still today I wonder how it would have been growing up with my dad." Foster Hixon was 39 years of age at the time of his death.

"A short time later, there were sirens..."

The Last Time Ever I Saw His Face II

"The family had no choice but to deal with the cards dealt them," Hixon asserts. "The loss of my father's income really hurt us. No such thing as Food Stamps or Section 8 Housing back then. I think we certainly would have qualified." According to Hixon, older brother Richard, 15 years of age at the time of his father's death, "became the rock in our family." Hixon recalls that his brother helped as best he could financially with his paper route. Richard was saving money to purchase a tombstone for his father. Donnie's brother Gerald, 13 years of age, also worked a small paper route.

Despite being born a cripple with a partial club foot, Donnie's oldest brother, Richard, set a good example for the family. Even after operations and treatment, Richard Hixon lived with one leg shorter than the other, which necessitated different sized shoes for each foot. Determined to beat the odds, his highly determined brother walked the steps of the nearby football stadium countless times during his youth in an effort to strengthen his legs. By the time he entered high school, he not only won a spot on the high school track team and ran the 100-yard dash, but also became a starting pitcher on the Richmond

Academy baseball team that won the state championship that spring. Three days after Ben Hogan won the 1951 Masters Tournament, on Wednesday, May 11, Richard Hixon pitched five innings in a 17-3 victory against rival Boys Catholic, and also went 2 for 2 at the plate. Nine days later, a year and a half from when their father passed away, the Hixons experienced tragedy again.

After school on Friday afternoon, April 20, 1951, Donnie recalls, "... some of Richard and Gerald's friends were in our backyard working on their scooters and bikes in the old tin roof garage that was built on the ground with an open front. That garage was at the end of the narrow dirt driveway that ran on the right hand side of the house. There was a wire fence on that side that was covered with honeysuckle vines that welcomed the butterflies, bees, and hummingbirds each spring. Some of the boys were getting ready to go and collect their paper routes and others were shooting basketball. Richard and Gerald were extremely well-liked and the Hixon's backyard was a popular hangout. The year before, Richard had finally saved enough money from his paper route to buy a used Cushman motor scooter. He might have gotten a little help from my aunts. I remember that the color of the scooter was blue."

Late that Friday afternoon, Richard, hopped aboard his scooter, with friend Bobby Holland on the back, and waved to his younger brother as they pulled out of the driveway. A short time later, there were sirens — something rarely heard in the neighborhood back then. Something was drastically wrong. People dropped what they were doing in their homes and yards and from all directions went running toward the commotion. Ten-year-old Donnie joined in the chase, which led him down the street and across the main road, Walton Way, where he turned down Eve Street, not far from the Hixon's previous family home on Jenkins Street. As young Donnie made his way toward the flashing lights in the distance, his advance was halted by Keith Prince, Preston Sizemore, and other friends of his brother, who detained him from going the last three blocks to where the red lights were assembled.

As boys in the neighborhood held him back, Donnie's mind swirled, and in the midst of the commotion, he caught word of his brother's name in connection with an accident between a car and scooter. Then came the all too familiar painful, sinking feeling in his stomach, the same one he experienced as an eight-year-old when his father died. In a state of panic, Donnie turned and ran home, crying hysterically, as an ambulance headed in the opposite direction passed him en route to the scene of the accident. His mom received news of the mishap at the downtown Belk's Department Store where she worked, and was whisked to nearby University Hospital. There she found her son, Richard, in critical condition, and his friend, Bobby, in a serious, but not critical state.

Throughout the evening, Donnie and brother, Gerald, huddled in the family's Holden Street home, and waited for updated information on their brother's condition. Each time the phone rang, their hearts pounded as they bravely fought back their emotions to answer it. Most of the calls they received were from friends, neighbors and well-wishers. Richard Hixon was not only a popular kid in the neighborhood, but also in the Augusta sports community as a standout athlete on the state's best high school baseball team. With their teammate fighting for his life, the Richmond Academy team, with their minds elsewhere, lost their only game that season the next day. It was the last game in an otherwise perfect season. Richard had been scheduled to pitch that day.

The front page headlines in *The Augusta Chronicle* that Saturday morning in large, bold letters in two lines read, "Richard Hixon Injured Here in Motor Accident Friday." The body of the article read, "Richard

Hixon, 17, popular Richmond student and athlete of 1013 Holden Street, is in University Hospital in most critical condition. His riding companion Bobby Holland is also in the hospital with serious, but not critical injuries." The Saturday afternoon newspaper headlines read, "Two Youths Hurt in Crash." Donnie remembers "Reading that in the newspaper really scared us. Both write-ups in the two papers were basically the same in giving the details of the accident. Meanwhile my mom would call to check on us."

The rest of that day and another anguished night, the brothers agonized, kept vigil near the phone, and found it hard to sleep. Then late Sunday morning, after nearly two days of waiting, a car driven by relatives pulled to the front of the house, with their mother inside. When they saw their mom crying and being helped from the automobile, the boys rushed toward it, knowing the news would not be good. Crying uncontrollably, their mom collapsed in the brothers' arms, as she fought to utter the words the boys could not bear to hear, "Richard, your brother, has died."

"They say the good die young," says Donnie. "Richard was a good and special person. Gerald and I were already without a dad, now we would no longer have our rock, mentor, and beautiful big brother around anymore. Richard's classmates and friends had a nickname for my brother and sometimes called him 'Ricardo.' *There would be no Ricardo anymore; he was gone."*

Thrown 77 feet, 10 inches after impact with a car that ran a stop sign, Richard Hixon, a senior in high school, succumbed to severe head injuries, among others. As was the custom of the day, he was not wearing a helmet for protection. Friend Bobby Holland, sustained a broken thigh and body lacerations, and luckily, survived. The auto that hit them, careened off course, and turned over before it hit a parked car. "After word got out that Richard had died, Preston Sizemore, Johnny Owens, and other friends of Richard went to the hospital to visit Bobby Holland that Sunday afternoon. He had gained consciousness, but didn't know Richard had died. When they told him, they said he just started crying."

What 16 months earlier was a family of five, the Hixon's now numbered three; a mother and two young boys. "We were poor, money was scarce, and once again," said Donnie, "my mother was faced with the burden of where the money was going to come from to pay the funeral expenses! She still owed relatives for dad's funeral, plus hadn't been able to afford a tombstone-marker on his grave. She didn't feel right about relatives helping and taking responsibility of paying the bill. We were very thankful for relatives who came to the rescue and helped out with my dad's funeral. My mom's sister, Aunt Miriam, stepped up to the plate again and paid for Richard's cemetery lot next to my dad's so they would be buried next to each other. My dad's sister's husband, Uncle Herbert, paid $50 down and the funeral home agreed to go ahead and bury Richard and give our relatives some more time to raise the money."

Hixon recalls in vivid detail the funeral services for his dear brother, Richard, that took place when Donnie was 10 years of age: "The day of the funeral was Tuesday, April 24, 1951, and was held at Elliott and Sons Funeral Home on Telfair Street starting at 5 p.m. It was a familiar place to me, as I was there once before for my dad's funeral. I remember getting into the cars with our relatives and driving to the funeral home, and dreaded going through this again. I kept crying and asking, 'Do I have to? Do I have to look at him?' I hadn't forgotten looking at my dad. It was standing room only in the funeral home, and people were still coming. A lot of his classmates (mostly girls) and friends of mine would come up to me, crying and hugging on me.

"I remember seeing people coming out of the viewing room crying their eyes out after they had taken a final look at my brother. Then, before the services started it was my turn. They had to pull me in there. When I entered the room I could see my poor brother, whom I loved and was very proud of, lying in his casket. I cried my heart out the entire time. He had white bandages wrapped underneath his chin and up to his forehead. You couldn't see his ears because the bandages covered them up; only some of his face just above his eyebrows, cheekbones, eyes, nose, mouth, and chin were visible. I was really frightened as they pulled me over closer and lifted me up to say goodbye to my brother. I was hysterical as I looked in his face seeing his head bandaged up like that." Donnie recalls, "I was told later that while looking down at my brother's face I kept yelling, 'I don't want to say goodbye to him; please don't let him go anywhere; I don't want him ever to go away.' Finally I said to him, 'I love you Richard and I hope you go to heaven to be with our dad! Please tell him hello for me!' This was the last time I would ever see his face.

"After that they escorted our family into the chapel for services. As we walked in the chapel, those who had seats stood as we were being seated. There were other people standing alone on the aisles along each side of the wall, in the back, and outside the doors as there were no seats left. When this was over, as with my daddy, I watched them load Richard in his closed casket into the back of that black hearse. We got into cars and followed behind in route to Westover Cemetery located on the Hill to see him get buried next to my dad. I noticed after we got on Walton Way in the Frog Hollow community where he had many friends and teammates, a lot of people had gathered on the street and were on porches looking. Passing by slowly with the car windows down, we could hear as some hollered, 'we love you Richard.' Hearing that, and when we passed by Jennings stadium where his high school baseball team played their home games, the crying started all over again! When we arrived at the cemetery, I watched them unload his casket from the back of the black hearse, carry it and place it over the grave site under the tents. When the service started, a lot of nice words were said about him along with prayers, and then it was all over; all you heard was the noise of those chains lowering him down in his final resting place on this earth.

"Those chains were an awful cold chilling spooky sound. To me it meant he was gone! No more dad, and now no more brother Richard! He had a big turnout. It was reported that when the hearse reached the cemetery some were still getting into their cars at the funeral home located in the downtown area. After that, while they stood around and talked, I picked up rocks and threw them in the fenced in pond that was in front of their graves located on the other side of the road. I watched the rocks as they hit the water and watched the ripples disappear at the shore line, never to see them again, just like Richard. When I think about that day, I am reminded of a quote by Franklin Graham that says, 'Time is like a river. You cannot touch the water twice, because the flow that has passed will never pass again.' That pond was small and sort of in the center of the cemetery that had some geese and ducks in it. Not wanting to hit them, I was careful to throw away from them to see if they would go where the rocks hit. After that everyone got back in the cars and headed back home where a lot of our neighbors started bringing us lots of food."

"...answered my mother's prayer..."

Benefit Memorial Baseball Game

In the days and weeks that ensued, the Augusta community poured its hearts out to the family. "As it turned out," Hixon relates, "God stepped in and answered my mother's prayer regarding the funeral expenses." A committee of Richard Hixon's classmates was formed and the following Saturday, April 28, a benefit baseball game between Richmond Academy and Boys Catholic was staged to help the family defray funeral expenses. Boys Catholic High School coach Denny Leonard altered his team's schedule in order for his team to play in the benefit game. According to Donnie Hixon, another article in *The Augusta Chronicle* noted that in the previous game between the two ballclubs on April 11, his brother, Richard, pitched five innings in a 17-3 Richmond Academy win and went 2 for 2 at the plate.

The morning edition of *The Augusta Chronicle* of April 28, 1951 screamed in bold letters across the top of the page, "Richard Hixon Memorial Game at Jennings Stadium Tonight." The article read, "Got your ticket yet?' That's what the members of the Richmond Academy and Boy's Catholic baseball teams will be asking pedestrians on Augusta streets today. Tonight is Richard Hixon night." The article highlighted the efforts of "a committee, headed by classmates Nath Hayes, Bobby Baggott and Tommy Herndon and Academy students" who "got together and distributed tickets among the members of the two teams, and the drive was on." The tickets were sold at a price of donation only, and according to Donnie Hixon another newspaper article reported that a second run of tickets was necessary.

"Before the game starts," the newspaper article continued, "the boys have planned a brief ceremony. The two teams will line up along the base paths while the ARC color guard bears the colors forward to home plate. After a moment of silence, they will listen to Taps, echoed in the furthermost corner of the park from the pitcher's mound where Richard Hixon once stood." According to Donnie, in his memoirs, "When they played 'Taps'... Mom said people were crying all around us, and it also affected the players as well!" Hixon went on to say, "While I was serving in the Marines, the flag on base was always lowered at sundown as Taps were played. This would remind me of the "Echo Taps" played that night at the ballpark in 1951 honoring my brother Richard.

"I have the 8 x 10 picture that was in the *Chronicle* newspaper on May 1, 1951 that shows the two teams on the field before the game. The Richmond players are lined up from home plate to 1st base holding their gloves over their hearts with their right hands. In the middle of the line-up is an empty space honoring Richard. The Catholic players are lined up from home plate to 3rd base doing the same." Richmond Academy won the hard fought contest 13-12, but needed a three-run 9th inning just to tie the game. "In the 14th inning," Hixon recalls, "second baseman Jack Poppell knocked in the run to win the game for Richmond."

On graduation day for the Class of 1951, Donnie attended the ceremony with his mother, and brother, Gerald at Augusta's Bell Auditorium. It is the same venue where Elvis Presley and Little Richard would perform later in the 1950's. But this would be a somber occasion for Donnie and his mom. "...each time a student's name was called, the families, friends, and classmates in the audience would cheer and holler their names, as they walked proudly up the stairs onto the stage to receive their well-earned diplomas. I remember vividly when Richard's name was called. I watched my broken-hearted mom walk on stage as she wiped the tears off her face to receive his diploma. This time there was no cheering, clapping, or any celebration going on. There was complete silence at first, and then as my mom accepted the diploma, you could hear some in the audience crying, and you couldn't help but notice them wiping away their tears."

The graduation was hard for Hixon to sit through and is just as hard when he looks back. "I saw some other proud mothers around me wipe away the tears running down their faces when their sons or daughters names were called. The difference was that theirs were tears of pride and joy, and ours were tears of sadness! When the graduation ceremonies were over, as with all graduations, the students threw their hats in the air, as they hollered and celebrated. Watching that was very depressing for me, my brother and mom. There was nothing to celebrate, and no hat to throw! We did get a lot of hugs and a lot of 'you have our condolences and we are deeply sorry for your loss' or 'what a fine boy Richard was, and we are so sorry,' which did help and meant something. While parents, friends and relatives of the other students walked out joyously, my mom walked out of that building without her son, and Gerald and I without a brother, with only Richard's diploma... a piece of paper."

After graduation, the Hixons left for Westover Cemetery and a ceremony planned by the committee of Richard's classmates that hosted the benefit baseball game in April. Proceeds from the game totaled over $1,700 and paid for two tombstones at Westover Cemetery in Augusta. The one for Donnie's older brother read, "Richard Lee Hixon 1933-1951, Student, Athlete, and Friend." On its base was engraved, "Erected by the students of the Richmond Academy and The Junior College of Augusta." In addition, the thoughtful students bought a matching marker for Donnie's father that read, "Foster William Hixon 1910-1949, The Lord is my Shepherd."

Richmond Academy went on to win the first of seven consecutive state championships under legendary Augusta coach A. L. Williams that spring. Sixty-eight years later, on Monday, April 29, 2019, *The Augusta Chronicle* paid tribute to Richard Hixon and the 1951 Richmond Academy team in Bill Kirby's "The Way We Were" series, entitled "Musketeers faced tragedy in title run." The article notes that Hixon was an all-around athlete who also represented Richmond Academy in basketball and track. It featured the picture of the honor guard and teams from Richmond Academy and Boys Catholic High, as they paid tribute to their fallen friend and teammate in the memorial game played in Hixon's honor.

In the summer of 1951, the ARC baseball team advanced to represent Georgia in the Southeastern Championships against an assembly from six states. According to Kirby's April 2019 report, based on a *Chronicle* report from the bus ride to Montgomery, Alabama, the team sang happy, jubilant songs — with the exception of "The Lord's Prayer," a hymn they sang on every bus ride, and also at their teammate Richard Hixon's, funeral. That night, Williams' ballclub huddled in a barracks at Gunter Field Air Base.

On the morning of June 21, nearly two months from the date of their star pitcher's death, Richmond Academy swept past Mississippi, and went on to rout Alabama that same evening 7-4 to lay claim to the

Southeastern title. According to Donnie Hixon, the Alabama team included future NFL Hall Of Famer Bart Starr. Rest assured, Richard Hixon was there in spirit as team captain Jack Poppell, who later played in the St. Louis Cardinals minor league system, hoisted the championship trophy, which now rests in a place of honor at the Academy of Richmond County. According to Kirby's article, the team left Montgomery "singing... Glory, glory to Old Richmond." ARC's baseball success was a bittersweet moment for the Hixon family.

After losing two family members in the span of less than a year and a half, times were even tougher financially for the remaining family members, Donnie, brother Gerald, and their mom. Determined to provide a Christmas for her sons, Donnie's mother scrimped and saved every penny she could that fall to pay for a bicycle, a nice shiny one, on a layaway plan from the local Western Auto. According to Donnie, she even went without lunch to put money against the layaway. Two days after Christmas 1951, her son proudly rode his new "set of wheels" eight blocks to the Rexall Drug Store situated next to Augusta's Allen Park. A section of the park was dedicated to Jennings Stadium, where Hank Aaron, among many stars of that era, would play baseball in the Class A South Atlantic League.

Located in "Frog Hollow," Allen Park was not situated in the best of neighborhoods. It was one of those areas where someone might see an unchained bicycle as a belated Christmas gift. That notion became crystal clear to Donnie when he exited the Recall Drug Store only to find out his bicycle was gone. Stolen! Crying, Donnie reentered the store to plead his case, but there was little that could be done except to file a police report. Determined to get his bicycle back, Donnie set out in the park in search of his treasured two-wheeler. But a band of three bigger boys that Hixon labeled as "bullies" chased after him. "While running from them," Hixon related, "I ran in front of a kid on a swing and got knocked down. I quickly got back up on my feet again, and started running as fast as I could toward the drug store. The bullies stopped chasing me and went away when I got inside the drug store. I was bleeding where the swing had hit me on the left side of my mouth just above my chin." Hixon said a lady in the store got him "bandaged up properly" and "made sure those boys were all gone." Then she watched as he walked for a ways as he "headed back home down the sidewalk, in the opposite direction of the park, brokenhearted and without my bike."

Hixon had the treasured gift for just two days. It was the only bicycle as a youngster that Donnie would own "as my Mom couldn't afford to buy another one." In place of the bicycle, Hixon sports a small scar on his chin that remains as a constant reminder of that day. "I felt really bad for my mom, and she and I both cried together when I got home and told her what had happened. She sacrificed and tried so hard to get me that bike and make me happy that Christmas so I could be like other kids on Holden Street who had bikes! It was hard watching them ride their bikes! Life just didn't seem fair! A lot of sorrow and anger was continuing to build up in me."

The Good Deed

On a hot July day in 1953 when Donnie was 12 years old, he performed a great deed, and his mom an ever better one! Donnie and friend Roy Booker had done some yard work for a neighbor in which their "compensation was going to be 11 cents apiece; six cents to buy a big drink, and an extra five cents to buy a Moon Pie — they were very popular back then... A Coca-Cola was only five cents and the bigger drinks like RC Cola, Pepsi Cola, Orange Crush, and other large drinks were a penny more. We thought what a treat and what a bargain!" As part of their wages, the boys would also be given two empty drink bottles for deposit, with the promise they in turn would return their soon to be empty bottles. It proved a shrewd business move that would save them two cents each on their drinks purchase. With their yard work completed, the two boys, soaking with sweat, walked the block, with those empty soda bottles, to a narrow "shotgun style" structure known as McMichael's Grocery Store, located where Merry Street abutted to Walton Way.

The front door of the establishment, according to Hixon, "was right on the sidewalk. Mr. Mac sat at the counter at the back of the store and could see everything going on outside. He knew who we were,"

Donnie attests, "as both families had been in that store a few times before, and Roy's mom traded there regularly." After Donnie and his friend paid for the sodas, they stepped outside, but before they had so much as consumed a sip, his friend, Roy, pointed to a man they recognized lying on the curb by the side of the road. Otis was "a middle-age muscular man of color who earned his money doing yard work and odd jobs, mostly for the rich folks on the Hill... Otis traveled around on his large bicycle which had a large wire basket attached to the handle bars. In that basket he hauled around his push lawn mower, a grass sling blade, a garden and leaf rake, and a pair of hedge clippers. That was about all you needed, and all anyone had in those days," Hixon recalls.

Otis had apparently gotten dehydrated after working a job on the Hill and fallen off his big bicycle across the street. Otis was in need, and Donnie gave the man his own drink that he'd worked hard for. "Roy let me share his drink and we sat down beside (Otis) until he finished his drink. When he was able to go, we helped him pick up his equipment which had fallen off his bike. He was very appreciative, thanked us, and left," Hixon remembers. "We returned the empty bottles to Roy's neighbor and told him what happened; he said he was proud of us for doing a good deed and being unselfish. I also remember that good feeling that I had for helping someone. Mr. Mac apparently didn't view it that way. About a week later, Roy's mother sent him to buy a loaf of bread. I happened to be at his house at the time and went with him. Mr. Mac let Roy come inside his store, but told me I couldn't come in his store anymore. Roy asked him why, but he would only say he didn't want me in his store anymore."

"I remember I went home with my feelings hurt very badly. I had no idea of what I could have done wrong, or why all of a sudden he didn't like me anymore. I was just a 12-year-old kid and didn't understand!"

When his friend related the incident to his mother, Mrs. Booker placed a phone call to Mr. Mac, who informed her that Donnie had taken something from the store without paying and would not be allowed back. Mrs. Booker in turn related the story to Donnie's mom, who suspected otherwise and "who then grabbed me up and we walked around to his store. When we got to his store she was very upset with him for accusing and treating me this way, and she wanted to know why. She was not going to leave that store and was determined to find out the meaning of all this. He finally told her the real truth. He told mother I helped and gave a n***** my drink! My Mom got in his face, cursed him out, and told him she was not raising her son to hate anyone, black or white, or any nationality, that we were all God's children regardless of what color we happen to be! I heard her say some curse words I never heard before! On the way out she turned over a tall bushel basket of butter beans and told him he didn't have to worry about me ever coming in his store again. Wow!"

“...a heap of athletic talent...”

Glory Days

In the 7th grade at Joseph R. Lamar Elementary, Donnie was a hard-charging running back. That same year, 1953, Burt Reynolds was Florida All-State in high school and signed to play football with Florida State, the same time that Ray Nitschke was on his way to play football at Illinois. The three would swap stories of those days some 20 years later. Though Donnie's mom didn't save any of his newspaper clippings from that season, "Joe Sheehan, a friend of mine," says Donnie, "gave me a copy of a game when we beat Monte Sano Elementary 26-0. It said I scored two touchdowns, and that teammates Ben Cheek and Brigham Woodward each scored one."

At the conclusion of the football season, Hixon transitioned to the basketball court where he played for Lamar Elementary as well as on YMCA and Biddy League teams. "Big he-man Stanley," as Hixon described Stanley Jenkins, used to ride three team members on his bicycle "from Joseph Lamar school to Chafee Park, located in the heart of the Harrisburg neighborhood," relates Hixon, "which like Frog Hollow, was a rough place. Benny Cheek straddled the handlebars with his feet propped up on the front fender. Brigham and I rode on the seat over the back fender."

A heap of athletic talent rode on that bicycle to Biddy League basketball practice. Cheek attended Georgia on a basketball and baseball scholarship and earned five letters in the two sports. Brigham joined him at Georgia "on a football scholarship and became a star on defense" and won three letters with the Dawgs between 1961 and '63. Hixon went on to fame in *The Longest Yard.* Another member of that team, Billy Marshall, left school to work and Jenkins quit school to join the Navy. A sixth member of that group, the only 6th grader on the team, Jimmy "Meat" Whitehead, earned All-State and All-American honors in football at Richmond Academy, was state champion in the shot put two years running and also played baseball. Then it was off to Georgia on a football scholarship, where Whitehead played on the line. He also proved a standout on the UGA track team. Whitehead was elected twice to the Georgia Senate, the first time in 2004 and again two years later.

To cap things off, Hixon's 7th grade basketball team at Lamar won the city-county championship and Hixon recorded 17 points in the title game. "We were the best, unbeatable! We were the champions!," exclaimed Donnie. "The good news," Hixon says, "is all my grammar school teammates mentioned are still living today and have been very successful in life." It proved quite a group of friends that Hixon surrounded himself with. Still, Hixon recalls, "In elementary school, during football or basketball games, sometimes I would look over to the sidelines and see someone's dad or brother watching the game and cheering them on. Right away I would tell myself how lucky those kids were, and I would lose focus on the game because I was thinking how I missed my dad and big brother. I was not able to hide from those tragic memories."

Summer of '54

During the summer of 1954, after the 7th grade, "we got a used washing machine. I remember it was round, open at the top with rollers... I thought we died and went to heaven when we got that washing machine with a wringer on it! The machine had a sticker on it saying keep your hands and objects clear of the rollers." Of course, boys being boys, "My brother Gerald used to play around and stick his hand inside the rollers. Once, he went a little too far before he could pull his hand out in time, causing his right arm to be pulled into the rollers. He was very lucky a friend was there with him to reach down and unplug the machine before he received serious injury. Gerald suffered some bruises on his upper arm. He never did try that again."

Hixon recalls that on rainy days and in winter, "We would hang our clothes out to dry on the clothes lines located on the screened in back porch... In the summer we... had clothes lines in the back yard. Other times, depending on the weather, we would hang them over chairs or wherever. Having a washing machine meant no more washing and scrubbing on a scrub board in the kitchen sink and bath tub. I washed most of my clothes, and I was good at ironing, plus sewing if needed. I was always conscientious about my clothes, and took pride in taking care of them..." Donnie Hixon's clothes were "organized, neat, and clean. I am still that way today. I was glad I was like that, as that was a big plus for me while serving in the Marines!"

All too soon, summer ended. It would be the last summer that he and his brother, Gerald, a rising senior in high school would spend together. "It was an exciting time for me when it was time to go back to school in 1954. I was starting the 8th grade as a 13-year-old teenager," and would attend Tubman Junior High. "Before school started, my Aunt Sara came down from Macon, Georgia, to help mom buy my brother and me some school clothes, notebooks, pencils, paper, and whatever school supplies we needed." You'll remember Donnie's Aunt Sara as the one who bought him the outdated, bargain-priced pants that caused quite a stir back when he was in the first grade. Still, Hixon relates that, "Aunt Sara was my dad's older sister who never had any kids, and who always had our back. She was our 'ace in the hole' in helping out whenever the situation really got bad. During those times, money was scarce and mom could use all the help she could get."

The Dungeon Awaits

In the spring of 1955, when Donnie passed to the 8th grade, his brother, Gerald, graduated and got married in short order. Gerald had played football at the Academy of Richmond County, or as it is better known locally, Richmond Academy. There he played on the same line as Nat Dye, the older brother of future Georgia great and Auburn coach, Pat Dye. The Dye brothers, Wayne, Nat, and Pat were each two years apart, and all three were football standouts at Richmond Academy and the University of Georgia. Between 1954 and 1960, the brothers combined for nine football letters at Georgia. The middle brother, Nat, played seven seasons in the Canadian Football League. The youngest of the Dye's, Pat, was three grades ahead of Donnie in school and was a two-time All-American in college. Pat played three seasons in the CFL with Edmonton, then for the Ft. Benning "Doughboys," where in 1964 he was named Armed Forces MVP. Afterwards, he began a nine-year stint as an assistant under Bear Bryant at Alabama, followed by head coaching positions at East Carolina, Wyoming, and Auburn. Pat Dye's disciplined approach to excellence fueled four SEC titles in 12 seasons with the War Eagles. Later in life, Donnie Hixon became best friends with Wayne Dye, the oldest of the brothers.

When Gerald left to start a family of his own on the other side of town, Donnie was especially lonely, and the summer of 1955 proved tough on him. His mother worked long hours each day at Belk's Department Store downtown, six days a week, with Sunday as her only day off. The 14-year old Hixon was on his own the majority of the day. The camaraderie that Donnie and his older brothers shared in that room on Holden Street could not be replaced and it took its toll on the youngest of the three. "I missed my brothers teasing, picking at me, and wrestling around with me," said Hixon. There was no male role model left in the house anymore to take me under their wings to inspire and motivate me." Without his brothers and father at home, Christmas of 1955 was just not the same for Donnie, then 14 years of age.

"I hated to go home when school was out knowing my brothers were not there. When I got home and walked inside, I would be welcomed by a home that had no happiness," related Hixon. "There was always a very lonely feeling for me when I entered that house, especially when I knew no one else was at home; coldness, sadness, and I would be haunted with sad memories..." Donnie relates, "Except for my mom, I don't remember getting any encouragement from anyone." Without male mentors and role models, Hixon's grades in school began to slip, and in no time he was failing at Tubman Junior High. School was no longer a priority.

"When I was going to have a test the next day, hadn't studied, and without much sleep because of bad dreams, I would be too tired to go to school the next day. So," Hixon continued, "I would play hooky and hide behind the tin garage in the back of the house until mom left to go to work," Hixon related. He knew something was missing in his life. "I was lacking the motivation, coaching, encouragement, follow-up, and the push to make education a priority that I used to get from my brothers. My big brothers, who were my heroes and mentors, were not around anymore and I missed them.

"I did have three good friends in Teddy Fulghum, Roy Booker, and Buddy Heath, who were all some of the most loyal friends anyone could have," Hixon relates. "When I wasn't around them, I would catch pigeons in a hay barn located nearby in the middle of a corn field across from Paine College. Daniel, the caretaker for Paine, would let me go in the barn and catch some. I had a large wire pen in the back of our tin garage that I kept them in. Somedays before feeding time I would let them out, they would fly around and come back to eat. Sometime there would be one that wouldn't. When there were no friends around, I shot a lot of basketball in the backyard or went over to Central Park. Donnie says, "It was still hard to believe we started out with five family members when we moved in that house, and at this point there were only two left living in that house: me and my mom. She was all I had left.

"During that year in the 9th grade, mom started dating! She would come home from work, usually with a man, on a Saturday, see to it that I had something to eat, and then go out on dates drinking and dancing. Sometimes," Hixon recalls, "she would come home after one o'clock in the morning. I didn't like this, or seeing her with another man, but I tolerated it and never said anything to her. Maybe she could see it in my body language. Most of the time those men would wait outside in the car." That especially irritated Donnie. "Can you believe that some were too good to come inside and showed no interest in me!" Like her son, Donnie's mom tried hard to keep going forward and put the past behind them. "Going out drinking and dancing," says Donnie, "was my mom's way of trying to bring closure to the tragedies and to escape that shadow that hung over her head from all of it."

"...the best present my mom could give me was a big hug..."

The Right Prescription

"After the holidays were over and 1956 was here, in January it was time to go back for the second half of the school year. My interest in school wasn't there anymore." While thumbing through a drug store magazine, an advertisement for a physical fitness course caught the 15-year-old Hixon's attention. "It was about a correspondence course from the "Jowett Institute of Physical Culture," a 12-lesson course that I got my mother's approval to take." Though his mom was financially stretched, she agreed to finance the inexpensive 12-lesson plan in hopes it would provide her son with something, *anything*, to look forward to! To put it mildly, the program proved life-changing. The goal-oriented correspondence course focused on breathing, self-defense, muscle development through the use of bands and isometrics, among other exercise-related material.

"This turned out to be the something I needed to get back on track," Donnie related. "I learned if I wanted to get results, I had to put the time and effort in, and I must be disciplined in sticking with and completing each course consistently in a timely manner. These were all habits I was missing when it came to paying attention in class and completing homework." Donnie's mom saw that her son didn't mind putting in the hard work necessary for improvement. He learned focus, determination, and follow-through, and embraced the "enthusiasm breeds enthusiasm" motto the course instilled. Upon the completion of each lesson, Donnie would send his mom's hard-earned money in the mail for the next installment of the program.

In March of 1956, when he turned fifteen, "the only and the best present my mom could give me was a big hug, telling me she loved me," Hixon relates. "The extra little money she had went toward paying for that course. With no extra money and no car, we never were able to go out to any restaurants like the families and kids today are privileged to... It was very depressing during Easter because I watched some of the other kids in the neighborhood, all dressed up, going to church with their parents in their automobiles! Watching them was very depressing, and was starting to make me jealous, angry, and it put a chip on my shoulder!" With the discipline the mail order course instilled, Donnie's grades in school were back on the upswing, but his efforts proved too little, too late. A failing grade in English forced him to repeat the 9th grade. According to Hixon, "It was getting hard for me to understand why I kept on having bad luck, and why I didn't see this happening to other kids in the neighborhood around me."

Throughout the summer of 1956 Donnie immersed himself in the Jowett Institute's physique building regimen, and by August, when he received his correspondence course diploma, he could pound out 100 push-ups without stopping, a half-dozen or so on each arm. He could also complete 25 dips between two chairs, do 10 or more chin-ups, walk on his hands, and tumble. "Since completing that course," Hixon says, "I've continued to focus on and maintain my fitness, which is still a top priority until this day. I benefited greatly and still apply many of the lessons and exercises I learned."

The correspondence course left Hixon lean and mean, and he approached his repeat of the 9th grade with a more positive attitude. He felt things would be different for him going forward and when football practice commenced, Donnie was ready mentally and physically, and showed promise on both sides of the football. But before summer practice's concluded, Donnie's football season came to an end. "In a scrimmage with the Richmond Academy B varsity," wrote Hixon in his memoirs, "I broke a bone in my foot and played on it by running on my heel for the last quarter. I knew it hurt me, but I didn't know the bone in my foot was broken." After the scrimmage, an x-ray of the foot showed a light break. As a precaution, the doctor put a cast on my foot to wear for the next four weeks, gave me a pair of crutches and sent me on my way. Junior high schools only played six games back then, and even if the cast came off and no more crutches, there would be no way I could be in shape to play in the last two games."

The foot healed in time for basketball season, and Donnie's favorite coach from his school days, Mutt Bearden, installed him as team captain. Also, says Donnie, "a pretty cheerleader by the name of Diane West caught my eye and became my first girlfriend. Our basketball team beat several high school B varsity teams and went undefeated in winning the Richmond County-City championship. In addition, we defeated the North Augusta B varsity team across the river in South Carolina. The majority of our players were out of the Harrisburg and Frog Hollow neighborhoods. There were no sissies on our team," says Hixon. "We did have some bad boys!"

"How could she do this to me?"

Say It Ain't So, Joe

The following summer of 1957, when Hixon turned 16, his mom married a man named Joe whom she had just met – *and he had never met Donnie!* Donnie walked into the house one Saturday morning after spending the night at the home of friend Butch McDaniel, only to find out the two had gotten married and that he and his mom were moving into Joe's house – *that same day!* "When I heard this I felt like a dagger went through my heart, and I kept asking myself, 'What would my dad and Richard think of this? What would my brother Gerald who didn't live with us anymore think of this? How could she do this to me?' She married a strange man I hadn't ever met and didn't even know, and now I was really confused about life!"

Before the initial shock wore off, Donnie found himself at Joe's brick house, on Martin Lane located on the Hill, replete with hardwood floors, modern appliances, and heating and air conditioning. These were things he was unaccustomed to, but being the team player he was, he adapted rather quickly. Aside from the shocking, sudden change, Donnie Hixon was in "Hill heaven!" His new "digs" were a far cry from his prior surroundings just down the road in the

Harrisburg section of town. Toss in two stepbrothers 10 years younger than Donnie, and in one afternoon he was part of the proverbial instant family.

Better yet, another cheerleader, the blonde, beautiful, and sweet Judy Trulock, who also happened to be in the same grade as Donnie and attended Langford Junior High, lived just across the street. Could life get any better? It could certainly get worse, and did rather quickly. No sooner than Donnie was getting used to the good life on the Hill, things took a quick reversal. Just a month after moving in, there were arguments between the newlyweds. Not long after that, a serious domestic quarrel nearly turned tragic until Donnie rushed home to find Joe holding his "mom by the hair and slapping at her." With blood running from her nose, Donnie's mom was crying as she attempted to fend off the assault.

It was all Donnie needed to see. Before he was through raining punches on his new stepfather, it was Joe who sported a shiner, busted lip, and bloody nose. When his mom and friend, Roy Booker, pulled Donnie away, Joe ran next door to call the police. As per police orders, Joe was sent packing for a week, as Donnie and mom collected their meager belongings. Within the week, they were back living at the bottom of the Hill, in a furnished duplex at 1003 1/2 Holden Street. The new address was just five houses up from the tragedy-ridden home at 1013 Holden Street they had moved out of just weeks earlier. It had all happened so quickly!

Goodbye, pretty cheerleader. Goodbye to the so-called good life. "I did get a taste of how the rich folks on the Hill lived for a short while," Hixon recalls. "I should have known living in that neighborhood was too good to be true." When they moved back to their old neighborhood, Donnie's mom confided she'd married because "she thought that it was chance to make a better life for me and her." Looking back, Hixon says, "She was really doing it for me." A year later the marriage was fully dissolved, but not before the next family crisis, just several days after the move back to the Holden Street neighborhood.

“...in a state of hysterics...”

Fight For Survival

Freshly settled in familiar surroundings, Donnie was awoken in the middle of the night by his mom, in a state of hysterics. "Come see Richard, he's in the living room," his mother beckoned to her son. "Look, your daddy is here also... look at them, Donnie," she shrieked. Unable to convince his mother that his father and brother were not actually there, he tried to awaken her from what he surely thought, hoped really, was a bad dream. When his mother did not respond, he reached for the telephone and dialed 0, summoned the operator, who in turn sent an ambulance. When it arrived, Donnie watched as his mother was placed in a straitjacket. Before the ambulance sped away, the driver assured Donnie over and again that his mother would be fine. Despite the reassurances, Donnie's stomach sank again, the same way it had when his father, then brother died in quick succession when he was just a youngster. As he walked back toward the house that the mother and son resided in for less than a week, Donnie Hixon at 16, now for the first time, was truly alone.

The following day, Donnie received information from his Aunt Grace that his mother had suffered a nervous breakdown and would be hospitalized for electric shock treatments to be administered. Furthermore, the therapy called for her to be sequestered at the hospital for two weeks, without visitors. It was apparent that the mounting stress of the past decade had weighed heavily on his mother, and the cumulative effect proved a load too hard for her to carry.

The toll was also shared by her son, and according to Hixon, he cried himself to sleep each night, and wondered if he'd ever see his mother again. Her absence also reopened old wounds from the time his brother Richard was in the hospital and didn't make it back home. Alone, Hixon was left to fend for himself for two long weeks, with no money coming in for groceries. Now in his late 70's, Hixon is still haunted with horrific nightmares from the stress endured during those 8 years of his young life beginning with his father's death.

In his new home for only a week, and his mom cordoned off in the hospital, the drama only intensified for Donnie when he heard commotion in the neighborhood. "I saw police cars and an ambulance arrive in front of the brick house across the street," said Hixon. "Soon after the paramedics went inside, they brought this lady out on a stretcher who was covered with blood, mostly all over her face." According to Hixon, a single mom apparently had a court order that prevented her father-in-law from seeing his granddaughter. The grandfather, armed, entered the house and shot the mother in the kitchen of the small house. "I don't remember hearing if the lady died or not," said Hixon. "Holden Street was a nice middle-class neighborhood where you wouldn't expect a shooting to happen!"

When his mother finally was allowed to go home from the hospital, Hixon said, "She looked like she had been through hell and back..." The episode had "caused her to lose a swatch of hair in the middle top of her head about the size of a silver dollar. Plus there were electrical burns still visible on her body." It was weeks before she could could return to work, and according to Hixon, the first two weeks at home it was as if she were in a stupor.

According to Hixon, "This was the same treatment the woman who had multiple personalities in the movie *Three Faces of Eve* received." Coincidentally, the Hollywood movie starring Joanne Woodward made its theatrical debut September 18, 1957 at the Miller Theatre in Augusta, mere blocks from where Donnie's mom had been hospitalized just weeks prior to the film's release. The movie was based on the book written by Augusta native Dr. Hervey M. Cleckley, and associate Dr. Corbett H. Thigpen, doctors of psychiatry and neurology in Augusta, who also aided in writing the screenplay. *The Three Faces of Eve* centered on a patient of theirs from nearby Edgefield, South Carolina, Christine Costner Sizemore. Woodward won an Academy Award for her portrayal of character Eve White in the movie.

"Thank goodness," says Hixon, "this barbaric procedure for treatment is rarely used and allowed anymore. That nervous breakdown... was caused by the stress of trying to raise me as a single parent, the grief over loss of loved ones, worry, and all she had been through. The pain she suffered finally caught up with her. That short marriage to Joe may have been "the straw that broke the camel's back."

To make matters worse, there was no safety net in place in the 1950s to help families in need. "Even then as a very young kid, I knew it was put up or shut up time for me," said Hixon. With rent coming due and no money coming in, it was in the summer of 1957, just prior to 10th grade, that Hixon took a part-time job to help his mom with the bills. "I realized it was all up to me now! The weight was all on my shoulders. That weight and pressure took a toll on my mom and attributed to her nervous breakdown, and I was determined it wasn't going to get me. I would fight to the end and survive!"

"...required to hustle at all times..."

Friends at Fat Man's

A gesture of kindness by good friend Buddy Heath saved the day for Donnie and his mom when they were down on their luck, had no income and were at their lowest point. With the help of his friend, a new chapter in Donnie Hixon's young life was about to be written. Heath put in a good word for Donnie at his place of employment, Fat Man's Sanitary Curb Market, Augusta's go-to produce outlet of the day. "This store was located in the middle section of Augusta where customers came from off the Hill and all around the city to buy groceries, fresh produce, and fruit." Afterwards, Heath subsequently stepped away from his own job at the corner market in order that Donnie could be employed. "What a true unselfish friend he was in giving up his job so they could hire me! Now that's a true friend! That was the kind of person Buddy was." Horace (Fat Man) Usry and wife, Carolyn, took Donnie under their wings, and according to Hixon, "...set examples I took with me the rest of my life, on how to successfully operate a profitable business, starting first with customer service." In short order, Hixon could weigh groceries and learned the fine art of social interaction with customers, and also how to upsell them.

Donnie "was required to hustle at all times" during his shift at Fat Man's. Of all the lessons ingrained in the young teenager, it was the Fat Man's advice, "Donnie, don't rush, *but hurry every chance you get!"* That mantra has served Hixon well to this day. "Believe me, making that a habit came in handy when I joined the Marines and all throughout my working career! He also said 'the customer is your best source of advertisement!' Today looking back, I would say to them 'Thank you Horace Fat Man and Carolyn Usry for teaching me some valuable habits and lessons.' I really got lucky working for them and being around all the other employees on my first job! Waiting on old and young, black and white customers helped me develop some much needed social skills also." Donnie Hixon hustled, and with his first paycheck was able to pay the $50 rent on the house that July of 1957.

"While working at Fat Man's during that hot, humid summer in 1957, summer camp for football at the high school started and I wouldn't be going out for the team with my friends Butch McDaniel, Billy Harris, and others. This was a big disappointment!" When school started that fall at Richmond Academy, Hixon worked evenings at Fat Man's, and also on weekends when needed. " At the end of the school day, I would do my homework, be at work at 4 p.m. and work until 10 p.m. at night." After closing the inside store, Hixon says "I would walk back to the house three blocks away down a pitch black dark McNally Alley. Sometimes mom would save me something to eat, or I would make a sandwich, eat and get ready for bed, wake up the next morning and walk to school four blocks away. Having to work and help out my mom, and give up high school sports was not an option for me. I had no other choice, but to *play the cards dealt me*, all the while trying to keep a positive attitude, which was hard to do, considering all my mom and I had been through!"

Even when his mother returned to work, hospital and doctor bills outweighed her income. "All the dreams I ever had of entering the 10th grade and playing high school football were destroyed... what a big disappointment and setback it was in my life..." At reunions Hixon is often asked why he didn't play football in high school. "It becomes very embarrassing sometimes having to explain the reasons, which further reminds me of my past," relates Hixon. Not being with a group of friends on a daily basis would impact him the most. "Instead," says Hixon, "I came away lacking those much needed social skills, and would go through life carrying a chip on my shoulder."

"A few days after school started, I ran into my junior high coach, Mutt Bearden, who had left Tubman for an assistant coaching position at Richmond Academy. He approached and asked me why I wasn't going to play football. With regrets I explained to him my situation, that I had no choice but to get a job and work to help put food on the table and help my mom. He said he understood, hated I wasn't going to be playing, and he admired me for taking on that responsibility at such a young age."

Kids from three diverse areas in the Augusta area fed into Augusta's Richmond Academy and tended to associate with those where they were from. "I was 16 years old in 1957 when I entered high school, and right away it wasn't hard to recognize what school the three junior high kids came from," says Hixon. No longer part of the Hill crowd, Hixon fit in best with the Tubman kids he'd grown up with. "Some of the Langford kids from the Hill may have had a car, and if not, their parents rode them to school in expensive Cadillacs. If you drove a Caddy back then, you were considered to be rich! Plus most of the kids from the Hill were easily identified by their nicer clothes and shoes. The kids from Murphy came on school buses from out in the county. The kids from Tubman were from poorer families and mostly walked to school."

The year prior to Hixon's start of high school, the Richmond Academy team captured the 1956 Georgia High School championship. Led by soon to be Georgia great Pat Dye, the Musketeers completed an undefeated season. A formidable athlete in his own regard at Tubman Junior High, Hixon wanted most of all to be part of the Richmond Academy's high school football tradition. The closest he would get was the produce market at Fat Man's. "The curb market where I worked was only five blocks away from the football stadium, and on football nights I could hear the roar of the crowd when something good happened."

In Hixon's words, "The 50s were a glorious time for... all teenage kids, but for me that was not the case. It was the start of rock and roll, country, and... great singers white and black. I did enjoy the music, but not the good times my friends were having in high school attending parties, having girlfriends, and hanging out... Most of all I was not able to attend Friday night football games where the stands would be full with high school students fraternizing, connecting, and cheering on their team. I was missing out on all of this because I had to work and didn't have the time for any social life!" While Hixon was going about his work schedule, classmates were with friends, going to school dances, or Teen Town after the games. The Varsity Drive-In across the street from Fat Man's, teeming with kids his age, driving their cars in and out provided a constant reminder of the good times he was not a part of.

"Anger set in, and the chip on my shoulder got bigger... (My) high school days turned out not to be the best days of my life as they were meant to be," says Hixon. Six decades later have done little to soothe Hixon, who still seethes when he thinks back on his high school experience. "I missed out and I'm still pissed off about it today when it crosses my mind!" The only consolation for Hixon is that he stepped up and put family first. "Making that decision to help my mom was worth it. To me, she was the best person in all the world!" It was a hard lesson to learn, especially for someone so young, and according to Hixon, "...sometimes in life, it isn't what you want to do, but what you have to do... you have to buckle your chin strap and just do it."

The structure that Hixon so desperately craved in his life came in the form of the military training he received his first year in high school. "Richmond Academy was an ROTC (Reserved Officers Training Corps) school. ROTC was mandatory if you were a male, and that class was called MST (Military, Science, and Tactics). You were required to take ROTC for at least one year. We wore an itchy wool uniform three days a week — Tuesday, Wednesday, and Thursday — and drilled all five days during the week. I didn't know it then, but I would benefit from this later when I joined the Marines."

The cruel lessons that life can offer continued in just his second week in high school when Hixon was challenged by an upperclassman during lunch. "School lunches were 25 cents and an extra carton of milk, which I always got, was 5 cents more," Hixon recalls. "My mom always made sure I had lunch money. There were no free lunches back then... This particular day I sat down on the very end of the table and took my first bite of food when this kid (this asshole) sat down directly in front of me. While he placed his tray down on the table, he leaned over my tray and sneezed all over my food." Donnie felt obliged to take a stance, to stand up for himself as he had been taught. His mom scrimped every day for her son's lunch money for many years and now Donnie knew what it was like to work hard for that money.

"I told him he would have to buy me another lunch as his friends and the other students seated down from us started laughing," Hixon recalls. The older student responded, "What if I don't, what are you going to do about it?" The upperclassman got up and came around the end of the table where Hixon was seated. Donnie stood up and greeted him, and as they stood eye to eye, Hixon said he politely asked again if the student was going to purchase him another tray of food. A firm "no" was the response, to which Hixon struck him with a thundering right to the side of the head. "He stumbled down to the floor, and I left the lunch room making a smart-aleck remark to his buddies, 'I bet he won't sneeze on anybody's lunch again.'"

Following lunch, Hixon was promptly summoned to Principal Markert's office where he offered an explanation of the events that transpired. "He said I should have reported this to the teacher on lunch room duty instead of punching him." Hixon responded to the principal, telling him that "my mom didn't raise me to be no tattle tale." He continued to plead his case, saying that the boy "sneezing on me and my food was no different than if he had spit on me, and that I wasn't going to let nobody get away with spitting on me. He still didn't have any sympathy for me, and expelled me for a week... When I returned to school a week later I was called into his office again, and he told me I busted the kid's ear drum and should be ashamed, and I had better not get into any more fights.

"That was nasty and disgusting what he did, and he shouldn't have. If I had told on him I would have been labeled as a tattle tale, or a chicken for sure by those other kids, and there would have been other fights." To this day, Hixon maintains he took the right approach with the situation. "I still stand by my actions that day as I sent a strong message to him and those other kids that you better not mess with me." None of the students at Richmond Academy targeted Donnie Hixon from that day forward. "They got the message! The culture I was raised in was, you got to stand up for yourself, even if it means fighting! Also, had I told on him, would the lunch room teacher on duty have offered me another lunch, or given back my mom's hard-earned money? Probably not! As far as I was concerned, I was the victim who got expelled, and had to leave school hungry without any lunch."

Life for Donnie that first year in high school was hardly ideal for a teenager whose life had changed drastically. A popular student and life of the party through middle school, Hixon became a loner and introvert. "With all that had happened in my life to this point, there was no fun, laughter, and happiness left in my heart!" That Thanksgiving of 1957, while others his age had time off for the holiday, Hixon worked the graveyard shift at Fat Man's, and took on full-time duties, from 9 at night until 6 in the morning. At 11 p.m. each night, Fat Man's closed its indoor store, while the outdoor store area remained open. As Donnie manned the outdoor area, the Pit Restaurant next door and the Varsity Drive-In, across the street from Fat Man's, also closed at 11 p.m. on weeknights.

That left 16-year-old Donnie Hixon alone to run the curbside business for the next five overnight hours, with a cash register situated midway between the main store and the nearby road. The fear of being robbed was always in the back of Hixon's mind as he went about his work detail long after midnight. Sometimes, he would recognize a friendly face, and for the moment, the fear of being robbed would recede. "I still can't imagine how at that young age I made it through all of this," relates Hixon.

"On rare occasions, a customer would come by that I would recognize, R&B legend James Brown! He showed up few times, usually after 5 a.m. with some of his band after an out-of-town performance in the Augusta area. He would get out of the car smiling, and was always friendly. I would always bring up about his hit song 'Try Me' that was such a big favorite with kids. You know the rest of the story. He became very famous, and was named The Godfather of Soul." Today, James Brown has a street, a statue, and an auditorium named in his honor in Augusta. Hixon has the memories.

Donnie cleaned out old fruit and vegetables from the bins and lifted full bushel baskets to replenish the staples, and waited on the occasional late-night customer. The only shelter and rest area availed Hixon was a 4-foot by 4-foot shack that stood 8-feet tall, similar to the old-style telephone booths that were popular back in the day. The tiny makeshift structure was situated along the sidewalk, next to the road, and afforded a small window so he could monitor the produce stands and the cash register located between the tiny lean-to and the main store. Inside the shanty was just enough space for a small heater, radio and old-style telephone, ones with the rotary dialing feature that might actually take longer to place than a phone call itself.

"Working there," says Hixon, "was always a very spooky place to be at nights after the streets were cleared, and it was rare to see anyone else out after midnight, especially during the week nights. It would get very quiet, and I would get a little nervous and scared being out there on that corner, with the cash register sitting out in the open, between the sidewalks, in the middle of the locked front door of the store entrance, just a few feet from the street. I admit the fear of being robbed did cross my mind quite a few times! I was well aware during those wee hours of the morning, of the danger and fear of being robbed! This was always in the back my mind, especially when a lone car would drive up and there was nobody else around. Only me, and the cash register that had very little money in it. I was a sitting duck!"

Just a 10th grader in high school, the situation proved overwhelming at times for a youngster his age with so much responsibility. "I was very lucky nothing bad happened to me!" exclaimed Hixon. "I was so very young in dealing with all of this. I was determined not to let fear, disappointment, and tough times overcome me. I still reminded myself I had no other choice, because I knew I had to work and not let my mother down. She needed my help. We needed each other. I knew I had no other options but to tough it out. All of this had an effect on my life no doubt. I learned a lot from all of it."

From the time he was a youngster, Donnie had an immense fear of storms that bordered on obsession, and working the graveyard shift at Fat Man's did nothing to quell the angst. He weathered many a storm in that lean-to, as it swayed back and the forth in the wind. "I remember one night in the summer while working there, a terrible thunder storm with high winds hit about 2 a.m. It was pouring down rain from a storm that produced large size hail that bounced up off the pavement only a few feet in front of me, and pounded hard on the tin roof of the small shelter I took refuge in. Those lightning strikes made me awful jumpy and put chills up and down my spine...

"...Then, out of nowhere a lightning bolt hit a transformer knocking out the electricity, Hixon exclaims, "and scared the living shit out of me! The transformer that exploded had fire shooting all out of it and was just across the street from me. The loud explosion the transformer made would scare anyone. To make matters worse, it was pitch black all around me after that and I had no flashlight. I was all by myself. Imagine all of this at my age. There was no traffic or people around that time of the night." While the lightning strikes continued, he remembers, "I stayed crouched down in that little shack, frightened, and kept praying and hoping I wouldn't hear any sounds like the roar of a freight train that would indicate a tornado was happening. Being that young, I admit I was scared out of my mind that night trying hard not to panic."

While classmates rested comfortably in their beds and in the safety of their homes, Hixon was left to fend for himself as he worked alone outside at Fat Man's throughout the night. When he did rest, it was in that shanty, abutted along the curb, and affixed with a hard wooden board as a seat. "I still remember being all sweaty during those miserable hot, humid July nights out there. I did have the luxury of a slight breeze from a large ceiling fan located in the middle of the walk area." On winter nights when the temperature dipped below freezing, he wore two pairs of socks to beat off the effects of the cold concrete floor, and huddled next to the tiny space heater. At least in summer, he didn't have to attend classes.

When school was in session, Hixon put in his nine-hour overnight shift, hustled home for a few precious moments rest, then made his way to school for the day. Only after a full schedule of classes at Richmond Academy was he able to head back home and catch a few hours sleep before the cycle repeated itself. He had long since given up attending high school events with friends whom he now felt disconnected with, especially on Monday mornings, when the talk turned to weekend activities. "I didn't have a social life anymore," Hixon maintains. "Working all night six and sometimes seven days a week, then going to school and hearing talk in the hallways and lunchroom about parties, football games, dances, and all the good times they were having was depressing!"

Hixon shied away from conversation he once thrived in and became more introverted. "I definitely missed out on all the good times the other kids were having! Working that job and attending school was tough on me." Donnie maintained the schedule for an entire year before he called it quits — in school. He gave up on his goal of a high school diploma to focus on being an employee at Fat Man's.

Fat Man's also proved an outlet for his pugilistic tendencies. Hixon never started a fight, but if provoked, would strike like a rattlesnake.

His father taught him at an early age the same lesson Burt Reynolds' father instilled in his son — "strike first and be the last man standing." Easier said than done maybe, but in Hixon's case, it was a move he perfected to a science, and even when he did not get off the first salvo, his lightning-quick reflexes, coupled with an instant shot of adrenaline, fueled his fists to a stellar outcome. It is what one could expect from a desperate sixteen-year-old forced to fend for himself without the aid of someone who had his back.

One night, after he had finished sweeping and cleaning out the curb in front of Fat Man's, a car with a pair of teenage couples drove by and deposited trash and beer cans at his feet. Donnie promptly cleaned up the trash and mixed it with a hearty supply of aging fruit and veggies to be thrown out at the conclusion of his shift. Hixon mixed a bucket full of the concoction, along with the contents of some leftover cola drinks near the produce stand. Then he stirred the slop together with the end of a broomstick. "The thought of pissing in the bucket crossed my mind," says Hixon, who promptly made his way to the teens' car in the back of the Pit Restaurant parking lot next door, where the couples were making out.

"The driver side window was down and his back was to me as he was busy kissing the girl on the passenger side," Hixon recalls. "I tapped hard on the side of the front door. The driver turned around and said 'What the hell do you want. Get the f*** out of here' Hixon says he kept the bucket in hand just below the open window and "I answered his question with 'I hate to break up your party,' after which I threw the rotten stuff through the window with the contents landing in his hair, face, and lap. That nasty mess went all over him and inside the car! Some of the stuff landed on his girlfriend's clothes, face and hair. When the two girls started screaming, I heard his friend in the back seat scream 'What the hell is going on?' As I was walking back to the front of the store I could hear him still cursing back there yelling out 'I'm going to get you, you son of a bitch!'"

Hixon had more than evened the score. "Soon afterwards, the teen in the front seat came around to the front of the store soaking wet with that shit all over his clothes and in his hair. He was a mess and pissed off! The others were standing behind him when he got in front of me shouting 'I play football and I'm bigger than you, you asshole, and I'm going to kick your ass, grocery boy!' He made a big mistake putting me down and calling me 'grocery boy' in front of those girls and the other kid, like I was a nobody. That was probably not the best word combination for Hixon to hear at the time. The asshole part, Donnie could handle just fine. But coupled with the words "grocery boy" was a phrase that Hixon could do without. Already oozing of low self-esteem, and already with a major-league chip on his shoulder, being put in the nobody category didn't quite suit Donnie. "I was going to make him regret making those remarks! I knew I had to nail him a good one," Hixon exclaimed "and I did just that when he got the words grocery boy out of his mouth!" Hixon greeted him with his best "Sunday punch," the one his father had taught him. Poor guy never saw it coming. According to Hixon, "Those girls and the other guy helped his bloody butt up, and walked him to his car around the back of the restaurant." Hixon remembers that, "When they left I got a bucket of water and washed the blood off the sidewalk." No need for Fat Man's patrons to get squeamish at the sight of blood.

Some two hours later, at about 4 a.m., according to Hixon, three cars pulled up in front of Fat Man's. First in line was a police car, followed by the vehicle that carried the youngster with his broken nose bandaged, along with his father this time. The three remaining teens pulled up in the third car. The father of the youth that had been injured requested that assault and battery charges be lodged against

Hixon. After hearing both sides, the police officer separated the two girls from the group and pressed for the truth. Hixon remembered, "Those two girls were shaking all over as he put a scare in them." A clearer picture emerged. The officer deduced that he could cite the teens for throwing trash in the street and underage drinking, and that the football boy with the bandaged nose had threatened Hixon. The father of the boy was told that he and the group of teens should leave before he changed his mind. Hixon's unprovoked boxing record now stood at 2-0 with two knockdowns.

"...punches full of bad intentions..."

New Year Cheer

The Christmas and New Year's holiday of 1957 and 1958 came and went without much fanfare. Donnie's mom worked days at the department store and Donnie continued to work nights at Fat Man's. It would not be long before Hixon was involved in more altercations during his Fat Man's tenure, including a Saturday afternoon bout at the Varsity Drive-In next door. After picking up his weekly paycheck, he ran into Buddy Heath, his friend who helped him get the job at Fat Man's, and Buddy's friend, Sherwood Lindsey. The three teens headed next door to the Varsity for lunch. Heath dropped a nickel into the jukebox and made his selection, only to see a teen seated nearby shake the jukebox until the tune stopped. Then it happened a second time. Hixon decided he'd make a selection. He meticulously chose James Brown's hit single, "Try Me," that Hixon had heard sometimes provoked fights. This one did too, though the selection likely wouldn't have mattered.

As Hixon stood and faced the jukebox, three of the other teens' friends grabbed Donnie from behind, held his arms and put a choke hold on Hixon, then spun him around. The fourth teen, the one that had shaken the juke box to stop playing music, pummeled Donnie with punches full of bad intentions that bloodied his nose. His only defense was to kick wildly at the youth until the establishment's owner intervened. As the youths were escorted out the door, Hixon informed the one who had thrown the punches that "...there will be another time, another place, you can count on it." Donnie Hixon was a man of his word.

Several months later, at around closing time at the restaurant next-door to Fat Mans, Hixon's friend, Buddy Heath, rushed over and advised him that the youth who had thrown the punches awhile back, was eating at the establishment. Donnie requested that his friend return and let him know when the youth was about to pay his check prior to leaving. It was only then that Donnie promptly discarded his hat and apron and scrambled to a spot between the restaurant's entrance and the young man's car. When the teen approached, Donnie asked him, "Do you remember me?" The youth said he wasn't sure, so Donnie jogged his memory, "and reminded him about being jumped by him and his three buddies from behind at the Varsity." In Hixon's own words, "Just before his 'lights went out,' the youth replied 'oh, yeah' with a smile on his face." According to Hixon, "That's when he took a hard right from me splitting his nose open before he landed on the pavement." Hixon stood above him and asked again, "do you remember me now?" After he kicked the youth in his private area, Hixon said the teen responded, "Yes, I'm sorry, I'm hurt, let me up, and I've had enough."

A half-century later, Hixon ran into this one-time foe while drinking coffee at the Books-A-Million store in Augusta. According to Donnie, "He was sitting across from me and kept staring." Finally, the man asked, "Are you Donnie Hixon? Do you remember me?" Only when the man pointed to a large scar across the bridge of his nose did Hixon recognize him. "We sat around after that laughing about it." The two combatants from their youth reminisced about the "good old days" when Fat Man's and the Varsity Drive-In were two of Augusta's premier destination points, and they were teens working out frustrations in their lives.

Hixon remembers that birthdays came and went for him as a youth without much meaning. "Springtime came around on March 21, 1958, and I now was 17 years old. Big deal! The future still didn't look any brighter for me, and I had no goals, passion, or direction in life. No mentor," he recalls. But his prowess as an enforcer spread quickly. The month after his birthday he was involved in another unprovoked dustup, this time at the Pit Restaurant to the opposite side of Fat Man's from the Varsity Drive-In. According to Hixon, the establishment was getting ready to close for the night, and a young man who was headed for Marine Corps training the next morning, had been drinking with a friend and refused to leave the premises. The Pit's manager, Wayne Newton, paid a visit to Fat Man's and enlisted Hixon's aid in getting the man to leave. Hixon says he politely approached the man and requested he leave so the workers could clean the joint and and call it a day. The future Marine responded by telling Donnie he'd leave when he was good and ready. Not seeking a confrontation, Hixon headed back to work at Fat Man's.

A short while later, the man showed up at Fat Man's looking to brawl and according to Hixon, picked up a couple of tomatoes and threw them in the street. Then he took a big bite out of a choice apple at the curbside market. Hixon informed the man, "you got to pay for the tomatoes and the apple." The angry man "rushed at me swinging wild, only to catch my best punch, and get knocked down. When he got up he didn't want any more! My fight record at the store was now 3 and 0." With three knockdowns. The Marine-to-be left with a bloody nose but not before he promised Hixon a rematch after basic training at Parris Island, South Carolina. Turns out, he too, was a man of his word.

Some five months later, after basic training at Parris Island, coupled with Infantry School at Camp Lejeune, North Carolina, the new Marine, true to his word and in fighting shape, showed up in search of a rematch. After a few beers at the Pit that evening to get good and loose for the bout, the newly minted Marine headed straight to Fat Man's, where the unsuspecting Donnie was knocked down from behind. "I never saw him coming," Hixon recalls. The next thing Donnie knew, he was on the cement floor of the outdoor market, wrestling with the man. Several bushels of fruits and vegetables already lay scattered on the floor in their wake. When Hixon got back on his feet, he gave the Marine what he termed "a terrible beating." Hixon's assailant had to be helped off the floor. "I give him credit," Hixon recalls, "for being a lot stronger, and he did put up a good fight in the beginning. He was no pushover." Hixon's curbside record at Fat Man's was at 4-0, and his amateur mark was 5-0 if you count the fight with the upperclassman at Richmond Academy High School. All unprovoked, each bout ending in a knockout.

As he headed into the 11th grade in high school, the grueling schedule of manual labor, six and sometimes seven nights a week at the market, coupled with school during the day began to take its toll on the 17-year-old Hixon. There were no parties, football games or dances for him to attend, only the seemingly endless grind of work and school, followed by more work. Even worse for Donnie was overhearing all the fun things he missed out on in the school hallways. "Still today," says Hixon, "there are no happy memories for me to reminiscence about my high school days!"

The "school of hard knocks" that Hixon attended was far removed from anything his classmates would encounter in school. Take for example the November night when Donnie was told by the store manager at Fat Man's to "be cautious and suspicious of any stranger who may ride up, as an armed robber had killed a police officer, and was on the loose in the area." Several miles away, and two hours earlier, "Sheehan's package store at the top of the hill on Wrightsboro Road" had been robbed. "Being a young kid I didn't want to hear that," says Hixon. "He told me to call the police immediately if you suspect anyone. I thought to myself that if I was getting robbed, I don't think the robber is going to let me call 'time out' to make a phone call. Yeah, right! I remember telling the manager 'I'm not going to the phone, I'm running like hell, he can have the money and the store.'"

Shortly after 8 p.m. and prior to Donnie's shift at Fat Man's motorcycle "Officer Frank 'Hank' Wall, Jr., who had a wife and two kids, stopped a vehicle in the 1300 block of Walton Way," within eight or nine blocks of Fat Man's. "Being suspicious," Hixon later found out, "Officer Wall pulled his pistol as he got off his motorcycle. The assailant exited the stolen car he was driving and fired a .32 caliber pistol six times." Officer Wall was critically wounded and the assailant abandoned the stolen car only blocks away (from Fat Man's). Patrolman Wall was taken to University Hospital where he died two hours later, roughly the time that Donnie reported to work that night. Hixon maintains that he was fine until "the inside of the store closed and the other employees had left, the restaurant next door and the Doo Wop Varsity Drive-In across the street closed. It got quiet and spooky. It was then that it all sunk in and I did get a little scared when I thought about it."

Hixon's attention was piqued late that night when a police car pulled up with blinding search lights that scoured the location. Two officers exited the vehicle and reiterated to Hixon that he "be on the lookout, we got a murderer on the loose who is armed and dangerous, and who we know is now on foot in the area. He shot and killed a fellow police officer!" Hixon remembers saying, "oh shit" to himself, and that he "wanted to close up and go home. But I couldn't," Hixon recalls, "as that part of the store stayed open, with no real way to close-up. I couldn't afford to lose my job! It wasn't until the police left," Hixon recalls, "when I really got scared... A couple of hours later, I was real jumpy and scared when the night got really quiet, and nearly 'lost it' later in the night..." when he heard what turned out to be two cats fighting over food in trash cans in back of the nearby restaurant. The murder of Augusta police officer Walls remains unsolved to this day.

"After that," retorts Hixon, "I never felt safe being out there all by myself, and I admit I was more jumpy than before whenever a customer pulled up. After midnight, especially between the hours of 2 a.m. until 6 a.m. when the inside store opened back up." According to Donnie, "on a good night only one or two customers might show up." Except for a teenager whose back was against the wall as Hixon's was, would it hardly be worth the emotional baggage that was exacted upon him on a nightly basis.

The Showdown

In December, Donnie and his mom moved from the duplex on Holden Street to a small, but furnished, upstairs apartment at 1307 Baker Street. Then came the first really good news for Donnie in quite some time. His older brother, Gerald, financed a 1951 jet black Rocket 88 Oldsmobile for him with the Georgia Railroad Bank. Donnie worked seven nights a week during the Thanksgiving to Christmas holidays to make the remaining four monthly payments of $32 on the car. He felt especially proud seeing the payment book stamped "paid" each month, and on March 1, 1959, he made the final payment. Donnie Hixon had bought and paid for his first car! The day after the last payment, he and his mom moved again. Their new residence was a furnished duplex at 1918 Starnes Street, just two streets from the one-time family of five's home on Jenkins Street, and back in the Harrisburg neighborhood. It marked the fifth dwelling in less than two years in which Donnie and his mom resided. But now, Donnie had a car!

The elation of owning a car was tempered just weeks later when Hixon experienced a life-altering moment as he came face-to-face with the policeman who drove the paddy wagon the night his dad died. It had been nearly 10 years since his father's death and the years had not been good to the now elderly ex-policeman. According to Hixon, the man had "a big belly, was obviously out of shape," and walked with a pained limp as he exited his car at Fat Man's around 1 a.m. in March 1959 to pick up some produce. Hixon did not notice the man at first. "After the man bagged up the items he came to buy, I weighed them," recalls Donnie, "and when the total price popped up on the cash register I collected his money. When I handed him the grocery bags a strange feeling came over me." Their eyes locked and in an instant Donnie's mind flashed back to that night a decade earlier when he chased a paddy wagon down the dusty street until he fell, never to see his father alive again. In that split second, the pain and the suffering stretched open Hixon's lungs. His nostrils flared. Donnie knew.

Then the old man broke the deafening silence. "Son, I can tell something is bothering you, and it's obvious you don't like me. What is it?" In an instant Hixon pointed angrily towards nearby Holden Street and relived for him the fateful details of October 21, 1949, just blocks from where the two now stood. Everything about that night was indelibly etched in Hixon's memory. Every nuance of that night he could recall with clarity, the flailing nightsticks and flapjacks as his father was bludgeoned into submission by the Augusta police, as well as the faces of each of those who got a few extra blows in afterwards.

"What are you talking about?" shrieked the old man. "I told him I was just eight years old at the time when this happened," Hixon said, "and that he was the driver of the paddy wagon that drove my dad away, and he never made it back home! Because of the beating ya'll gave him, I don't have a daddy anymore!" Hixon bellowed at the man, "Ya'll beat him to death, and covered up the real reason why he died by saying he hung himself!" The old man stood before him in stunned silence. "When I told him my dad's name, Foster Hixon, the man just stared at me, and you should have seen the expression on his face. I was wanting him to say something, but he just stood there in silence and said nothing."

Each second seemed an eternity for Hixon. It was if he could peer into the old man's soul. Donnie's blood boiled with rage and and adrenaline coursed his veins as Hixon made ready to avenge his father's death. As he reared back to strike the elderly man, to pound him as his father had been beaten, Donnie somehow managed to hold back. He'd noticed something. Hixon watched as a tear formed and fell from one eye of the former policeman. Then the floodgates opened and he witnessed tears of remorse flow down both sides of the old man's face. "That told me he did remember," says Hixon, "and had guilt and regrets... the Good Lord must have been with me, in giving me the strength to get control of myself and not harm him." Donnie's demeanor changed in the blink of an eye from rage to pity. No words were spoken, yet each man understood the weight of the moment, the confession of sorts that had taken place. Then the elderly man turned, limped back to his car crying, and drove off.

"I had never heard a grown man cry like that" related Hixon. "That situation could have gone really bad, and I would have gotten myself in big time trouble! I'm so glad I didn't hit him! He was an old crippled-up man and couldn't have defended himself against me, and I would have gone to jail. Those tear drops streaming down his face and the crying got to me, and really saved the day," said Hixon. "I can still remember hearing him crying as he got into his car that night. Today, I am very proud of myself for not hitting him! I still believe today, no doubt, that God was watching out for me that night!"

"...wearing three days of stink..."

Here Comes The Judge!

The following month, April 1959, Donnie Hixon bought "spinner" hub caps for his car, all the rage at the time. He would soon find out that popular hub caps on a car parked at the back of a business establishment late at night would prove to be a problem. Later that month while working at Fat Man's, Hixon went to the parking area in back one night to move his car to the front, and realized the spinners had been stolen. A month later, acting on a tip from an acquaintance, Hixon took things into his own hands and re-stole what he thought were his spinners in the middle of the night from a car parked several blocks away. Big mistake! When he was arrested two days later, he found out the spinners he stole weren't the ones stolen from *him*.

On Friday, May 29, 1959, Hixon was promptly thrown into "the Bull Room" in the 4th Street jail in Augusta, "surrounded by a bunch of nasty stinking drunks and thugs." For the better part of three days he sat there on the floor, the youngest of those in attendance. On Monday, June 1, wearing three days of stink, Hixon was summoned to an appearance with a judge. When Judge Wesley Killebrew entered the courtroom smiling, Donnie was taken off guard. In this case, Judge Killebrew had done his homework and was aware of the misfortune that had befallen the Hixon family, and the sacrifices and strides Donnie and his mom made in the face of adversity. Just as Donnie felt a bit of relief and maybe even thought worthy of being bestowed an award, the judge shifted his glasses down and uttered the word *"However,"* and that changed everything. Hixon could feel his stomach drop as the judge completed his sentence, "...you made a bad choice in breaking the law and you can't go unpunished."

The judge excused himself, and upon his return an hour later, handed down a sentence to Hixon that proved to be a life changer for both Donnie and his mom. "Son, this will be the best thing for both of you," the judge said, as he informed Donnie that he had arranged for him to join the Marines. The shock jolted Donnie, as he uttered the words back, *"The Marines?"*

"Don't worry," Killebrew reassured Donnie, "you will make a good Marine, you are the kind they are looking for." In exchange, Donnie got a get-out-of-jail pass along with a clean record. The judge also arranged for Donnie's mom to be listed as dependent, according to Hixon, "thus making her eligible to receive a military allotment check each month and have much needed medical and dental benefits."

From the judge's chambers, Donnie received a police ride home, and just time enough to brush his teeth, shower the stink off, and get into some fresh clothes before a Marine recruiter paid a visit. The following day he packed his bags and spent time with his mother. At precisely 7 a.m. on Wednesday, June 3, 1959, Donnie Hixon's life changed forever. A polite, well-built, and handsomely dressed recruiter at their door greeted them. Donnie's mom was impressed. "Mrs. Hixon," the recruiter intoned, "the Marines are going to take good care of your son. Don't worry, he will be fine. It is the intention of the Marine Corps that upon Basic Training, he will be a different man, a better man."

With that Donnie gave his mom a goodbye hug. As the car pulled away, Donnie looked out the car window to see his mother crying on the porch – she was all alone. "That hurt," Hixon recalls. Five days from the time he was arrested and jailed, Donnie Hixon was off to the Marines. He boarded a Greyhound bus for Macon, Georgia, where he was sworn into the military. Then he boarded a train for Yemassee, South Carolina, where he took a Marine Corps bus to Parris Island, South Carolina.

"...the true challenge that lay ahead..."

Parris Island

Twice en route to being sworn in, Hixon was thanked for volunteering his service. On both occasions he answered back that he hadn't volunteered, that a judge back in Augusta had done that for him. Hixon didn't know the meaning of "Semper Fi" that day or the true challenge that lay ahead. His first night on the island, a drill instructor got the recruits' attention when he warned them, "Don't try to escape, there are alligators on this island. If you step on one in the dark it might bite your leg off. Not only that, poisonous snakes come out at night, and the island is surrounded by dangerous marsh land." Comforting thoughts for the young men to ponder. Upon completion of his first week of training, Hixon thought to himself, "Man, this was punishment, and was going to be a four-year sentence given to me by the judge!"

From the time he was awarded a certificate from the fitness course taken from three years earlier, physical fitness became a priority in Hixon's life. As he hoisted bushels of produce onto his shoulders during the lonely night shifts at Fat Man's, Hixon honed his muscles even more. But nothing like the regimen and results that the Marine Corps produced. The hell that Hixon endured over the course of three months at Parris Island molded him into a man, packed on 22 pounds of muscle, and left him more physically fit and mentally alert than he'd ever been. For the first time time in his life, he ate three square meals of the best tasting, highest nutritional value food and received physical and dental exams.

Throughout Basic Training, Hixon choked back his laughs as peers did the "duck walk" and what they could to keep Drill Instructors off their backs. When it was his turn to report to "the hatch," when the drill instructor told him to hit the ground and give him 20, Hixon pounded out 100 pushups. Instructors found out that Donnie Hixon was a fit Marine. Then, he too, like his peers, performed the "duck walk" for the DI.

Upon graduation from training at Parris Island, Hixon left as a proud Marine, a title he earned, not an entitlement bestowed. "Besides my mom and family, the Marine Corps, for the first time in my life, made me feel like I was important!" attested Hixon. "I can't say that for any (school) teacher I ever had! I also give credit and thanks to Judge Killebrew back in Augusta for looking out for me. He knew what was best for me, and sent me off in the right direction! God bless that judge!... Leaving Parris Island that day felt great, a proud feeling of relief and accomplishment! For the first time in my life, I felt like I accomplished something!"

Parris Island was the start of a four-year journey that would prove a blessing in Hixon's life. Next up was a two-month stint at Camp Geiger in North Carolina. Hixon knew there'd be more challenges ahead. "I could hear my mother's voice in my head... 'I taught you to be positive — you stay strong and remain tough — make me proud!'" At Camp Geiger's School of Infantry, Donnie learned "to shoot the .30 caliber Browning Automatic Rifle, (a.k.a. BAR), the .50 caliber machine gun mounted on tanks, throw grenades, gas chamber survival, (and) combat training at night..."

Then it was back to Augusta for two weeks leave, where he placed a phone call to his mom at Belk Department Store from the Greyhound Depot. "When I told her I was back, I was told later she let out a scream that was heard all over the store, scaring customers and employees, and kept hollering 'my Donnie's back!'" He took a cab to the department store, where Hixon recalled, "I was in my tropical uniform and was greeted by my mom with open arms, a hug and a great big smile, a smile I hadn't seen in a long time." Five months in the Marines had transformed Hixon into a new man. Just as the Marine recruiter promised her the day Donnie left for Parris Island, her son, now a rock-solid Marine, returned to her a different and better man. "The crying and sadness I saw on her face the day I left," Hixon remembers, "was now all smiles and happiness when I returned! A good thing, a blessing. Those smiles made it all worth it!"

Camp Lejeune's "Home of Expeditionary Forces in Readiness" was next on Hixon's itinerary, where he reported to Alpha Company of the 1st Battalion 8th Marines (A-1-8) of the 2nd Marine Division. There he completed combat and amphibious assault training. There would be other hurdles to scale as well, one in the form of a fistfight with a known tough guy under his command once Hixon was promoted to PFC.

Never one to start a fight, Donnie tried to reason with Marine in an effort to get him to pull his weight and work as a team. As Hixon remembers ...a lot of the other Marines had gathered around. I remember (the tough guy) said, "F*** you, I'm not doing shit," then paused, stared me down said, "What you going to do about it Georgia boy, run tell the Gunny?" Hixon says he responded, "Yeah," and was greeted with a roundhouse right that caught him off guard and connected to his forehead. *Strike first and be the last man standing was not going to work in this situation.* Hixon was rocked backwards and off his feet. "I saw stars!," Donnie said.

With adrenaline pumping through his veins, Hixon managed to roll over and was back up quickly as his assailant attempted to kick him. Hixon screamed to his opponent, "You son of a bitch, you ain't getting away with this shit." Once up, Donnie commenced a barrage of punches on his opponent, and in the end it was Hixon's speed and heart that won out. Hixon recalls that his opponent stopped fighting "and never came toward me, the fight was over." Most called it a victory for Hixon, but Donnie says it was a draw. It proved to be the fight of Hixon's life, against this Marine from Louisville, Kentucky, who reportedly trained out of the same boxing club as the great boxer Cassius Clay, as he was known at the time, and later as Muhammad Ali.

A bloodied Hixon earned respect for standing up to a bully that day, and gained a reputation as a fighter. Hixon was a hero in the barracks. "I remember my dad saying if the person you fought wasn't bleeding, or had a black eye, or both, you didn't win." Both men were bloodied profusely and Hixon sports a scar under his eye to this day. "He would have enjoyed watching that fight." According to Hixon, "Gunny Nogacek took a liking to me after that, and shortly afterwards promoted me to Lance Corporal." The kid from Augusta, Georgia, *Lance Corporal* Hixon, was on his way.

While at Camp Lejeune, Donnie's mom moved to Florida to live with neighbors from Augusta who decided to relocate to the Sunshine State. Later in Florida when Hixon had 14 months remaining in the Marines, she married Army veteran Leonard Kleskie, whom she had previously met in Augusta. He was a man Donnie liked and respected. His mom never had to work again. Later, when Hixon got out of the service and was working in the finance industry in Augusta, his mom and stepfather moved back to Augusta, and purchased a home in order that she could be close to both of her sons, Donnie and Gerald.

Hixon was motivated to continue his education and rarely "left the base on weekend passes," but spent his time hitting the books and exercising. In the fall of 1959, as his former classmates in Augusta headed into their senior year at Richmond Academy, a determined Donnie Hixon had already earned his high school equivalency in the Marines. Even after having dropped out of high school in his junior year to help put food on the table, Hixon made up for lost time and graduated nearly a year ahead of his Augusta classmates.

From mid-May through the end of November, 1960, Hixon sailed aboard the USS Chilton, crossed the Atlantic Ocean, went through the Straits of Gibraltar and into the Mediterranean Sea. Once there, the APA-38 attack transport ship that he was aboard conducted assault and landing exercises throughout the Mediterranean. The young Marine from small-town Augusta got to visit the great cities of Europe — Rome, Cannes, Athens, Malta, and Barcelona were just a handful of the points of interest during the itinerary. "It was an opportunity to see beautiful European women everywhere, especially the ones enjoying the sun on the Italian and French Riviera beaches. It felt very strange witnessing the different cultures in that part of the world." For a young man whose entire life was confined to Augusta, Georgia, and nearby locales, it was all very exciting. "I was mesmerized by it all," Hixon recalls, "and very thankful to the Navy and Marines for the opportunity to witness another culture, and be able to see that part of the world! Unbelievable!"

During his stay in the Marines, Hixon proved a standout athlete in all sports including boxing. Like he had at Fat Man's, Hixon maintained his unbeaten record in the military, both in and out of the ring. This is the friggin' Marines we're talking about, the best of the best! Donnie much preferred street fighting over the more controlled and protected environs of fighting in the ring. "You fight without gloves for a reason," Hixon says. Fighting in the streets brings "a different kind of fear. In a street fight you've got no referees and no protective gear and no one can stop the fight." According to Hixon, in the ring, with protective headgear on, "it's hard to draw blood, plus your opponent can quit at any time." In street fighting, the mano a mano type of pugilism that Hixon favored, there's blood and one man standing. That man was Donnie Hixon.

In March of 1961, Donnie received orders to report to the U.S. Naval Base in Bermuda where he would serve his final two years in the Marines."Right before leaving for Bermuda," Hixon relates, "I broke my right hand. I never lost a fight. I never liked fighting with gloves on, but I loved to fight bullies and smartasses in a street fight!" Throughout his life, Hixon had no respect for bullies that teamed up on weaker opponents. It all stemmed from seeing his father beaten by those four policemen at a tender age. Hixon left the Marines with a right hand that had been broken twice from the pounding he administered to opponents. To this day, he suffers from nerve damage in the hand and right arm. "Once stationed in Bermuda, I was involved in four more fights, and was a winner on all of them," says a slightly modest Hixon, "and became a hero among the good guys in the barracks." Over half a century later, on Friday, October 2, 2015, Hixon received an unsolicited e-mail from friend and fellow Marine Don Hillaker, from Michigan. "In Bermuda," Hillaker wrote to Donnie, "you were my hero. You were the only true Marine. You stood up to all the Marines. I am proud to serve with you."

In addition to his boxing prowess, Hixon played on the Bermuda Marine basketball team that posted a 30-1 record and was quarterback of the Marine football team his second year. In football, Hixon was mentored by Princeton great Francis Lovecchio, the bruising blocking back who paved the way for 1951 Heisman winner Dick Kazmier. The strategies he learned from Lovecchio he would incorporate to the Augusta Eagles semi-pro team after he left the Marines. Yankees legend Joe DiMaggio, and other greats visited the island. Hixon played football while in the Marines and played fast-pitch softball against Heisman Trophy winner Joe Bellino, who played for the visiting Navy team from the States.

On December 21 and 22, 1961, President John F. Kennedy met with British Prime Minister Harold Macmillian at the old Bermudiana Hotel, which was demolished in the 1990's. It was there that Hixon contends, "I got the surprise of my life." As Donnie exited the hotel where he'd just been relieved of duty, "here comes the Secret Service, or whoever they were, coming in with the President. I stepped aside, dead in my tracks, in shock as I fumbled to straighten my uniform hat while standing at attention to salute him. Very embarrassing! I was having a Gomer Pyle moment. I was caught completely off guard as they hurriedly walked by. I never expected to see him! He probably recognized I was shaken up, and as he (JFK) passed by he touched my shoulder and said, 'It's OK, Marine!' I only got a quick glance at him. No eye contact... A very distinguished, high-class looking person. If you didn't know he was President," says Hixon, "you just knew he had to be a very special and important person."

Playing sports and walking the beautiful beaches of Bermuda, Hixon somehow made it through those final two years of service, and soon enough his active duty in the Marines came to an end. The stint in the Marines changed his life and Hixon utilized the discipline he learned going forward. "I spent my last night on active duty at the Navy barracks in South Philadelphia packing my large Marine duffle bag, (a.k.a. Sea Bag) with all my uniforms for the last time," Hixon recalls. This was kind of sad for me, knowing I wouldn't be wearing them anymore, not to mention I was leaving some great Marine friends behind whom I probably would never see again." Still, Semper Fi and "Once a Marine, Always a Marine" would be relevant throughout the course of his life.

"I had successfully served my country for four years as a United States Marine," says Hixon. "I was very proud of myself! I had grown and matured as a man, was full of pride and confidence, and knew I was capable of facing the world...always thankful to the Marine Corps for preparing me for this day."

Before he fell asleep that last night of service, Hixon reminisced about his mom and deceased father, his deceased brother Richard, his older brother Gerald, and his journey in life that brought him to this point. Hixon recalled thinking, "I'm all grown up now, and very confident in knowing the Marine Corps had prepared me well. They definitely made a difference in me, mind, body, and spirit! I was coming out with a positive attitude, believing in myself and my abilities... When my last reveille sounded the next morning as an active duty Marine, I hit the deck with both feet raring to go."

The once misguided teen from Augusta, Georgia, Donnie Hixon attests, "The Marine Corps was a life-changing experience. The best teaching and coaching advice I ever received in my life was from the leaders and mentors whose path I crossed in the Marines!" In four scant years his life changed dramatically. Hixon had transformed into a rock-solid Marine, a man with purpose and self-esteem. For Donnie Hixon, things would be different going forward. "I would see to it!... Now it was up to me to take the life-learning lessons I learned in the Marines, use them, return to civilian life with a positive attitude, and make a difference in my life going forward by being a catalyst!" Hixon did just that upon his return home, and worked himself up in the business world, first as a manager of a finance and mortgage industry in Augusta, and then as an Assistant Vice President over the state of South Carolina, in addition to sections of Georgia, North Carolina and Florida. "The success I've had in life" Hixon maintains, "is because of my character development, discipline, and training I received in the Marines."

Hixon also retains a soft spot in his heart for Fat Man's, for lending a hand when he was a young man in need. The opportunity to work at Fat Man's as a young teen was not only a learning opportunity, but also proved a launching pad for Hixon. "When I returned home after four years in the Marines," Hixon remembers, "that part of the store (where he had worked as a teen) had a 12-foot high security fence around it, with a large gate in the middle, and another on the end. When the store closed at night, the produce section did as well. It wasn't cost-effective to keep it open, plus after I left, the outside was robbed a couple of times. It was just too dangerous for one person to be there all alone with a cash register sitting in the open." In short, finding another Donnie Hixon when he'd gone off to the Marines was a tall order to fill.

While the original Fat Man's remained in roughly the same location for several more decades, the company has since changed addresses and business models several times. The hard-work ethic and dedication to quality that Horace and Carolyn Usry instilled in the original version of Fat Man's continues to this day. With a second and third generation of Usrys steering its vision, Fat Man's remains an Augusta institution, and has continued to expand its brand into the 21st century.

"...events that would soon rock the city..."

The Sky Is On Fire

Monday, May 4, 1970, is a date that lives in infamy in American history. In the wake of mass protests and heightened tensions over the war in Cambodia, Ohio National Guardsmen fired into a group of protesters at Kent State University. Sixty-seven shots rang out over the span of 13 seconds. Four students were killed and nine others were wounded in the shootings. The university closed for six weeks. America was on edge.

Donnie Hixon also remembers May 4, 1970, as the date he underwent surgery at University Hospital in Augusta, Georgia, to remove torn cartilage in his left knee. Prior to the advent of arthroscopic surgery, the operation to remove the meniscus in Hixon's knee left him a five-inch scar down his leg. Three days later he was sent home on crutches with orders to "take it easy" for awhile. Hixon spent the weekend in rehab at his residence. The shootings at Kent State were top of mind in the news. Little did he know of events going on in Augusta that would soon rock the city.

On Saturday, May 9, 1970, a 16-year-old mentally ill black youth, Charles Oatman, was found brutally murdered in the Richmond County jail in

Augusta. City Councilman Grady Abrams subsequently viewed the teen's body at Mays Funeral Home, and his description of the corpse was disturbing. The back of Oatman's skull was caved in, his body was pocked by cigarette burns, and three deep gashes opened up the length of his back. At the funeral home, owner Carrie Mays heard that Oatman was administered the beating by two other black youths in his cell after a card game. The apparent rules of the game called for the player with the losing hand to be beaten.

The official sheriff's report read that Oatman sustained fatal injuries in a fall from his bunk after being hit. After viewing Oatman's body, Abrams didn't buy the story and neither did Augusta's black community. In the final analysis, two black cellmates were charged and later convicted in Oatman's death. But in the absence of that additional information, and an apparent coverup by the sheriff's office, rumors of wrongdoing spread like wildfire throughout the black community. By Monday, May 11, 1970, the inner city was in chaos.

Riots were the last thing Hixon had on his mind when he left his apartment that day. After a week of inactivity, and anxious to get a workout in, Hixon grabbed his crutches and hobbled out to his 1968 Ford Galaxy convertible, blue top over white. Nothing on the front page of The Augusta Chronicle that morning hinted of tension in the streets, nothing that would inspire Hixon to tune his AM car radio to WBBQ, Augusta's radio powerhouse. Instead, Donnie jammed his favorite Chuck Berry Golden-Oldies eight-track tape into the player mounted in his car and pumped up the volume. Then he headed to the gym at his friend's home, located downtown. Herbert Gilstrap lived with his mom on 10th street, who also owned the boarding house next door, where the gym was located. His friend was not at home when Donnie arrived, but Gilstrap's mom was, and luckily for Hixon. The music that emanated from Hixon's eight-track player muted the sounds of mayhem around him as the unsuspecting, and some might say oblivious, Hixon drove straight into a riot zone.

As he pulled alongside his friend's home to park his car, Hixon remembers hearing sirens in the distance, and other sounds that he dismissed as firecrackers. That, and maybe a celebration going on. Thinking nothing of it, Hixon cradled a crutch under each arm and headed around the back of the car when he "heard what sounded like multiple gunshots coming from the front of the Goodyear store on Broad Street." He turned to see a small group congregated in front of the store, and according to Hixon, "Some had guns and were shooting up a storm toward the other side of Broad (Street)."

It was then that he heard his friend's mom bellow from the front door of her house to Donnie, *"Get in here quick – there is a riot going on!"* Hixon recalls that some of the group started his way, while others were still focused on the other side of Broad Street. "I didn't panic" said Hixon, the former Marine, "(I) just had the sense of urgency 'to get my ass on the porch' and in(to) the house." In his haste to do just that, Hixon "stumbled over the stone curbing, fell down on the sidewalk (and) leaving my crutches, crawled up the stairs, where Mrs. Gilstrap greeted me... while handing me Herbert's shotgun."

Hixon admits that what happened next was a mistake on his part and if he had it to do over he'd have done things differently. "I immediately laid down," he said... "with the shotgun in the prone position, one that I was familiar with from my Marine training. I should have gotten inside and locked the door instead of lying down with part of my body and the gun sticking outside the door of the porch. It seemed like a good idea at the time, the right thing to do..." (But) "It was stupid of me being visible and in the open presenting a hittable target like that. It just might have been an invitation... (to) start shooting at me..."

According to Hixon, two members of the group spotted him with the shotgun and "took off running down Ellis Street," while two others threw guns, apparently out of ammo, onto the rooftop of the back of the Goodyear store. Hixon was lucky. The group moved on. "I hate to think about what might have happened if I had arrived a little earlier. You never know! I'm just glad it played out the way it went down." Hixon stayed at the Gilstrap house for about an hour until his friend showed up, grabbed his crutches and hobbled as quickly as his slowed body would take him, back inside his car. "...with the windows down I could hear a lot of gunshots, sirens, noise, and saw smoke in the sky from the downtown area! I hauled ass, running red lights and not worrying about a traffic ticket!"

Hixon floored it in the opposite direction of the mayhem, turned from Greene Street onto 15th, and roared over the Archibald Butt Memorial Bridge, all the way to Augusta's main tributary, Walton Way. When it was safe, he turned his trusty car radio up loud to monitor the AM radio chatter of what was happening downtown. As he sped up Walton Way it could not have been far from Hixon's mind that the section of town that was the center of so much pain in his life, this road leading up to the Hill, was now his refuge.

Acting on a plea from Augusta Mayor Millard A. Beckham, Georgia Governor Lester Maddox sent in 1,000 National Guardsmen, who converged on the city in the wee hours of Tuesday, May 12. The Guard was backed up by 150 Georgia State Troopers. Not one to call off on a sick day, later that morning Hixon headed downtown to the finance and mortgage company he managed. Located at 11th and Greene Streets, the office was situated just around the corner from the home he was holed up in the day before. Hixon recalls, "There were truckloads of Guardsmen and armored tanks patrolling all around the downtown area, and up and down Greene Street and Broad Street."

By Tuesday, May 12, *The Augusta Chronicle* finally paid notice to the crisis on its front page. The newspaper featured a photograph taken from North Augusta, South Carolina, of smoke that billowed above downtown Augusta to accompany the headline, "3 Dead in Augusta Riots; State Guardsmen Activated." Before it was over, six blacks died – all shot in the back – and scores of others were injured in three days of rioting. Governor Maddox reached out to James Brown and the renowned entertainer flew to the city from Michigan that afternoon to help quell the riots.

Brown owned a radio station on Eisenhower Drive, across the street and down the road from the Augusta National Golf Club, and it was there he met with Maddox. The two agreed that "Someone has to talk to the kids and the black community" and it was agreed that Brown had better rapport with the community. According to the newspaper account, "...the soul singer agreed to broadcast taped appeals to youth to cool their anger... and appealed to women and children especially to stay off the streets." Brown also called on the city's establishment to meet with leaders of the black youths and hear them out "about the problems and demands of the city's poor."

The Oatman case opened fresh wounds for Hixon, who was still haunted by the same question that wracked his brain since the death of his father two decades earlier. For Donnie, it was personal. As a young boy, Hixon witnessed the Augusta police bludgeon his dad, Foster Hixon, a white man, who died in police custody in October 1949. After the Oatman case, Hixon asked again, "...why did the police allow this to happen, and why did they lie to the hospital doctors how it happened?... That 'damn lie' (cover-up attempt) started a racial riot we didn't need in Augusta, costing many lives and property damage! Again," Hixon says, "not all policemen are bad – it's the few that sometimes give police a bad name."

"...I'll help you rob this place..."

The Great Escape

During the course of his young life, it seems that Donnie Hixon had more than his share of dustups. Such was the case one fateful day at the downtown site of Town Finance Enterprises, where Hixon was assistant manager at the time. On this particular day, a tall, black man, wearing a wig and dressed as a woman walked into the office. The Marine in Hixon immediately kicked in and Donnie hurried toward a supply door in the hopes he could work his way outside to summon police. But the shrewd assailant made a "Jackie Chan-like" leap over the counter to thwart Hixon's advance and stuck a handgun in Donnie's back. The man ordered all six employees to move in back of the counter and onto the floor. Then the robber knelt on one knee and pressed the barrel of his pistol between the eyes of store manager, Bobby Rogers.

Wired a bit differently than the rest, Donnie told the man holding the gun, "no disrespect, but I'm not going to lay down on the floor." Instead, after "pissing in my britches," says Hixon, "I told the burglar, 'Look mister, we just work for this company and *don't give a shit about them losing money – I'll help you rob this place, just don't hurt nobody.*'" To prove his point, Hixon yanked telephones out of the wall one-by-one and threw them over the front counter. He even told the intruder that when questioned by the police, hey'd say the person they were looking for was "a short Chinese-looking man."

As the assailant weighed his options, the barrel of his handgun remained stuck to office- manager, Rogers' forehead. Sensing that Hixon, the smooth talker with the strong Southern accent could be counted on, the bandit handed Donnie a rather large pocketbook with instructions to empty two cash drawers into it. When the drawers were empty, the robber demanded that Hixon collect everyone's wallet, but one worker, Mrs. Berry, refused to do so, crying out that *"little Milton's picture is in it!"* Hixon immediately snatched the wallet from her hands and screamed, *"The hell with little Milton's picture, Mrs. Berry! This man is holding a gun on us!"* Hixon then told the assailant he personally didn't carry a wallet, but kept money in his left front pocket. Per the assailant's instructions, Hixon carefully pulled out four crisp one hundred dollar bills, cash from the previous day's paycheck. "You are honest, I like you brother," the man disguised as a woman told Hixon.

Donnie was honest enough that the robber finally pulled the barrel of his weapon away from the office manager's face. "Donnie and I have always been close," says Rogers, but that day he saved my life... Had he not been there, he'd (the robber) have probably killed me." As the odyssey continued, the assailant focused his gun on the six employees and shepherded them into a tiny restroom at the rear of the store. Hixon says he stood atop the toilet in the cramped quarters as the group was instructed to count to 100. At the count of 50, the front doorbell sounded, still the hostages continued their count as instructed. When they opened the door, the group was shocked to see the assailant still standing there, with gun pointed back at them. It had been a test. Then the five were ordered to squeeze back into the room and begin their count a second time. This time, Hixon says, they counted to 500 before they had the nerve to peer out!

The following week, a bank four blocks down and one block over on Broad Street was targeted. When the robber emerged from the bank, an alert Augusta traffic cop, Leonard Wheeler, signaled other police from his motorcycle, who joined in a foot chase over several downtown blocks. The event culminated in a shoot-out at the Augusta Court House where the assailant was wounded and subsequently apprehended. Police believed the assailant to be the same man who robbed the finance company where Hixon worked. Though the suspect was thought to be the same in both robberies, he was convicted of only the bank robbery, and sentenced to 10 years, to be served at Georgia's Reidsville State Prison. It would not be the last time that Donnie Hixon and the man would meet face-to-face.

“If there had been an Internet in 1972, (Reynolds) would have broken it...”

Cosmopolitan

After years of toiling in obscurity, in 1972, Burt Reynolds, then 36, quickly came into the international stream of consciousness. "Women around the world," related Hixon, "and myself found out real quick who Burt Reynolds was after he posed naked and was featured in the centerfold of the April issue of *Cosmopolitan* magazine in 1972. This magazine was a very popular fashion magazine for women and had been on the newsstands since the late 1800s (a long time). This type of article was unheard of at the time and big news back in 1972. The famous photo showed him lying on a bear rug with only his left hand and wrist covering his private parts. He became the first male to pose naked in this magazine that gave all kinds of advice to women on fashion and beauty, sex advice, careers, health, self-improvement, and you-name-it."

The magazine was well-timed to hit the stands in April 1972, three months before the movie *Deliverance* opened and quickly sold out. Says Hixon, "After posing in the *Cosmopolitan* magazine Burt's popularity skyrocketed again when the movie *Deliverance* was released and shown in theaters across the country in July of 1972.

A quote I read somewhere," Hixon recalls, was that "If there had been an Internet back in 1972, (Reynolds) would have broken it."

"After the *Cosmopolitan* sell-out and the *Deliverance* movie had been out," Hixon recalls, those girls in my office always had big smiles on their faces whenever talking about how handsome he was, and that he's got it all..." Little did he know at the time that Hixon would one day cross paths with this international star in a way he could not possibly imagine.

Eyes on Eagles

The Augusta Eagles semipro team was the creation of Herbert Gilstrap, who came up with the idea after watching teams from the like-sized cities of Savannah and Charleston play. In 1967, the Eagles played only two games, winning both, against the Waycross, Georgia, Swampers and Greenville, South Carolina, Mountaineers. The team played a 10-game schedule in 1969, and Eagles head coach Cotton Frazier was replaced mid-season by Harvey Hogan and assistant coach Henry Dukes, a former Georgia Bulldog standout.

A standout all-around athlete in the Marines, Hixon was in the best shape of his life when he tried out for the new Augusta Eagles semipro team in the fall of 1968. And during his career from 1968-'71 Hixon played two years at quarterback. According to Hixon, Frank Gibbs quarterbacked the team during the 2-0 short-season first year, and Columbia County athlete Bobby Meybohm was over center the next two seasons. Hixon was at quarterback along with Charles Evans during the '71 and '72 campaigns and began a stint as the Eagles offensive coordinator in 1973. Donnie's older brother Gerald, the one that lined up alongside Pat Dye during their high school days in Augusta, was the team's head coach.

On a sweltering summer day in 1973, a phone call came to the Augusta Eagles football team that would change Hixon's life in a way he could never have imagined. At 32 years of age, his career as quarterback of the Eagles was behind him. But like Burt Reynolds and NFL great Ray Nitschke, Hixon, too, had one more game as a player still left in him. Enter Pat Studstill. The former NFL standout Studstill played four seasons at the end of his career for the Los Angeles Rams. The newly minted technical advisor, Studstill had been tasked by Paramount Pictures with finding the best recently retired NFL stars and semi-pro players in Georgia to surround Burt Reynolds in *The Longest Yard.*

Production was set to commence filming that fall at Georgia's maximum security facility, Reidsville State Prison. Oblivious to the happenings in the south Georgia town 110 miles south of Augusta, Hixon went about his life as usual, never dreaming what was about to head his way. With Deliverance now in his rear-view mirror, Burt Reynolds, Hollywood heartthrob and box-office sensation, began preparing for his next big project.

Studstill opened the Yellow Pages and placed a phone call to Information in search of Georgia's semi-pro football teams. Augusta came up first alphabetically. Studstill placed his call and Augusta Eagle owner Dr. Gus Carlucci answered. "Old smart Dr. Carlucci," Hixon relates, "who graduated second in his medical school class, wasn't about to tell the Hollywood producer that the Savannah Indians semi-pro team was closer to Reidsville. Savannah was only 64 miles away, versus 110 from Augusta. No sir! Doc had always dreamed of being in a movie." According to Hixon, "The doctor assured Studstill that Augusta was just a short drive to Reidsville..." He also confided in the Hollywood casting agent that he could deliver the rare player that could double for Burt Reynolds!

Studstill paid a visit to Augusta, where he watched the Eagles practice at Murphy Junior High, and penciled in players he felt he could surround Burt Reynolds with in the movie. The next day, Donnie recalls it being a Friday afternoon, when Dr. Carlucci phoned him at his office and revealed to him what the visit by the man from Hollywood was all about. Carlucci informed Donnie that Studstill would probably need around 15 players from the Augusta Eagles for *The Longest Yard*, and that "they were still looking for a stand-in double for Burt Reynolds."

Carlucci also confided that Studstill showed a lot of interest in Donnie and observed how he coached the offense at the practice. During that session, as Hixon had often done, he would get under center, bark out signals, and run a play to demonstrate to Eagles quarterback Jimmy Padgett how it should be executed. "I still had the urge to play," says Hixon. "After Doc told him I was a former quarterback, he told Dr. Carlucci there was a strong possibility he would consider me as Burt's stand-in. My office staff was standing around listening in on the call, and after he said that, I yelled out in a loud voice, 'me, a stand-in stunt double for Burt Reynolds in a football movie, you got to be kidding, what the hell does a stand-in do?'" Hixon was in seventh heaven. His office workers were in shock! "I didn't hardly know about Burt Reynolds," says Donnie. " I never went to the movies much. The girls in my office, they saw *Deliverance*. And then when his picture came out in *Cosmopolitan* magazine, I remember them talking about it."

Carlucci told Donnie that Studstill would be back with additional talent scouts at Butler High Stadium the following week for the Eagles home game against a semipro team from Douglas, Georgia – yet another team closer to Reidsville than Augusta. No longer a player, Hixon would be scrutinized on the sidelines, and the names and numbers of the players the film people might be interested in would be circled on their programs. According to Hixon,"*The Augusta Chronicle* writeup the morning of the game reported that the movie people were going to be in attendance, and that 15 or so players on the Augusta Eagles would to be chosen for the production." The article also mentioned that Donnie was being considered as a stunt double for 'Superstar Burt Reynolds!' I got a lot of calls from a lot of friends that morning wanting to know if this was true," relates Donnie. "All of this was a shock and hard for me to believe. I had doubts! I really didn't believe they would choose me. I asked myself why would they? This was just too good to be true!"

Hixon says Carlucci confided after the fact that "he knew he had to give his best effort in selling them on me as Burt's double once they showed interest. Carlucci told him I was an ex-Marine, and as a player, once punched an official out for laughing at a teammate when the game ended." He also told Studstill about "the time as a coach that he (Hixon) tripped an opposing player running down the sidelines, which caused a fight to break out... Studstill said Burt definitely would be interested in hearing all of this. Dr. Carlucci figured if they selected me," says Donnie, "then I would be the 'ticket' in getting himself, and the other players in...

"The night of the game," Hixon recalls, "the stands were full with spectators hoping to get a glimpse of the Hollywood people. During the game a man with an expensive-looking camera walked up and down the sidelines taking pictures... We knew all the sports writers from *The Augusta Chronicle* and this photographer wasn't one of them. We assumed he must have been associated with the movie people. Just before halftime the photographer returned to the stands. I was glad, as he was making me nervous and distracting the players... who were just hoping they'd be among those chosen. Maybe because of the distractions and lack of player concentration, the team didn't play very well the first half and went into the dressing room only slightly ahead. After a good talking to in the dressing room, the team came out the second half, played better, and won big!"

During the next few weeks, Donnie said he "received calls from friends, and some came by where I worked. I was approached wherever I went." Everyone wanted to know if he'd heard anything yet, and when he thought he might. "I told them all," said Hixon, "I wish the hell I knew." For someone who lived his entire life outside the spotlight, this was all new and exciting for Donnie, but was not without its drawbacks. "The pressure of getting asked about it was getting to me. Even the sports writers from the newspaper phoned, and always ended the call saying with, 'If you hear anything, call us right away.'"

When waiting on information, days and weeks can seem like months. "After a few weeks," Hixon recalls, "I was a little embarrassed, disappointed, and still had my doubts anything would become of this. I admit I did have my hopes up! Who wouldn't? One night while having a beer with friends at a local sports bar, we all were laughing about it, when one of them said 'Donnie, you don't reckon somebody has pulled Dr. Carlucci's leg?' Others joined in, 'yeah Donnie, you've been had!' Another one chimed in and said 'Donnie, I hope not, but I think this may turn out to be a should have, could have, and didn't happen situation! If so, it just wasn't in the cards for you, so let's all drink another beer.'"

Donnie tried his best from that point forward to put the entire situation about being Burt Reynolds' stunt double out of his mind. "...which proved not possible, as people continued in the days ahead to ask questions" about the potential of him being part of the major motion picture film. Not to be disrespectful, some asked, "Why would they pick you, when they could have their pick of quarterbacks right out of college?" It was a pretty good question and one that Donnie pondered himself. "We hope all of this is true," his friends would say, "and not a hoax, because you don't deserve any disappointment!"

It would be another long week of waiting before Hixon heard anything from Dr. Carlucci, and when he did, the doctor confirmed that a number of his teammates from the Augusta Eagles had been chosen to be in the movie. The doctor also related that he, Carlucci, had landed a speaking role in the film. Lastly, Carlucci confirmed that Paramount Pictures had chosen Donnie to be Burt Reynolds' stand-in. "Unreal," Donnie exclaimed. "This movie would be seen all over the world! Participating in this movie more than made up for having no social life, and not able to play sports or finish high school. Unbelievable! This would also help make up for the tragic struggles, countless letdowns and disappointing times I lived through before I joined the Marines."

Though Hixon was already in great physical condition, "Doctor Carlucci said the message for me was to be in tip-top shape. He said we would be receiving more instructions on when to report to the Reidsville State maximum security prison, where filming of the movie would be made." As it all worked out, the duo, along with members of the Augusta Eagles semipro team selected, reported to the prison three weeks later. Five years younger than Reynolds, Hixon was the full package. Young, athletic, and within a few pounds and inches of the movie star, when Hixon put on a football helmet, the two were nearly indistinguishable. Plus, Hixon had Reynolds' swagger and good looks, and more importantly, could take the pounding delivered by the likes of Ray Nitschke and bounce back to his feet.

The troubled kid who left high school to support his mom, Hixon would finally have his time in the spotlight. All the obstacles he had overcome in life prepared Hixon for the moment at hand. He requested a two-month leave of absence from his position as branch manager at a local finance and mortgage company, and hoped for the best. "The next morning," Hixon relates, "my supervisor, J.C. Carter, had driven in from Atlanta and was waiting outside the office door. He seemed more excited than I was!" Carter had contacted the owner of the company, whose headquarters were in Delaware, and the request was approved. A stellar employee with an impeccable work record, Hixon's higher-ups in the chain were so supportive of their model employee, they not only granted the leave, but paid Hixon in full during the nine weeks he was gone. "Working with Burt Reynolds?... You got to be kidding!"

Hixon felt the events unfolding before him had to be a dream. "It was the shock of my life, because I never would have figured why they wanted me. And I got in there, I reckon, by luck. And I was really kind of leery about doing it when they first told me. I thought it was a joke when they first approached me about it." And then there were the obvious concerns about working inside a prison that Hixon couldn't shake. "At first, this sounded very dangerous to me – what if a riot breaks out... Maybe that's why I got selected, because others turned my role down! Up until the time I reported to Reidsville, I thought the movie people were taking a hell of a chance – filming a football game inside the walls of a maximum security prison... would have to be very risky. What if we got trapped inside the walls of that prison when a riot happened to break out? There were a lot more prisoners there than us."

Married and with a small child, Hixon says despite concerns about working within the prison, it was an opportunity he simply could not pass up. "After weighing all this, I admit I did have some concerns, but never any second thoughts about taking part in the film. After all, I can't turn down a once-in-a-lifetime opportunity like this, one that doesn't come along everyday. I've got to go for it, it can't be that unsafe... As it turned out, the only person I would need to fear was Green Bay Packer legend Ray Nitschke, and not the prisoners!" It was fate that Nitschke's storied career ended just prior to the start of filming at Reidsville, making him available to play in five more weeks of scrimmages. Any frustrations that Nitschke had about retiring when he felt he could still play in the NFL, he would be happy to take out on whoever might oppose him. Being Burt's stand-in meant that it was Hixon who would take the physically punishing shots from a cast of former NFL greats, including Nitschke.

Donnie also tossed a hypothetical situation around in his brain. If the company he worked for had said no to his request for time off, "Would I have quit my job, or would I have told Paramount Pictures 'no?' That was a good question, and I'm glad I didn't have to make that decision! I would have not gotten a second chance with Paramount Pictures, and I would have had no problem getting another job. Now you know what my decision would have been! Everyone, including my wife, mother, brother, and friends all said in no way could I turn down a movie opportunity with a star like Burt Reynolds who was fast becoming the biggest star on the planet!"

Hollywood, Here I Come

During the day and into the evening before he reported to Reidsville, Hixon received phone calls from friends and well-wishers. Their message was the same. "We hope NFL all-pro linebacker Ray Nitschke don't hurt you too bad and break too many bones! I didn't get much sleep that night and tossed and turned most of the night. The next morning after getting packed, I was raring to get going on my way." Still the feeling of nervous anticipation in his stomach would not go away. "While driving down to Reidsville," Hixon relates,"I was real nervous and thought all of this must be a dream. Working with Burt Reynolds? You got to be kidding. Something this big just doesn't happen to you every day!"

The soon-to-be #22 Donnie Hixon, stunt double for Burt Reynolds, was giddy as he drove the 110 miles to Reidsville, Georgia, on a morning bright with sunshine. He let the feeling soak in as he traveled through the small towns, and communities with miles of farmland, "seeing all the miles of cows and horses in their green pastures." All the while, Hixon says he thought to himself, "I wonder what kind of a fellow is Reynolds? Believe it or not, I even thought about if he was an asshole and maybe we might not get along. I also wondered how I was going to fit in with those Hollywood people, and how would I feel about playing football inside a maximum security prison surrounded by some of the world's most dangerous criminals who were murderers, kidnappers, thieves and more."

Eager to get started, Hixon arrived in the small farming town of Reidsville several days in advance of most of the Augusta Eagles taking part. He arrived in the tiny downtown area around lunchtime and asked "what restaurant serves the best 'soul food.' lunches... I got directed to an establishment down the street, parked out front and entered... They were right. I thoroughly enjoyed that country cooking and the hospitality." Next, Hixon requested directions to the state prison from an "older man sitting outside the restaurant." Hixon says, "He pointed straight ahead, saying it was down the highway about five miles. I got into the car and drove the five miles, only to see a large white prison building that read, Citrus State Prison and not Reidsville State Prison. Out front there were a lot of 'Keep off Property, Danger, and No Trespassing' signs everywhere," Hixon related, "not to mention the large tall guard towers out front, and all the barbed-wire fencing all around. After seeing all of that, I traveled down the highway a few more miles in hopes of spotting a sign that would say Reidsville State Prison. There was nothing but swamp and farm land.

"Finally," Hixon relates, "I turned around, drove back to the restaurant, got out of the car and approached the old man, who was still sitting there." Perplexed, Hixon proceeded to inquire of the man,"Are you pulling my leg, mister? The only prison I saw on that road was Citrus State Prison, and nothing else..." To which the man replied, "Oh, I forgot to tell you, we got movie people from Hollywood in town who changed the name of the prison last week. They are going to be filming a movie there." Hixon felt slightly embarrassed. "Did I feel stupid or what! Somebody should have told me! How was I to know!"

So, the redirected and now thoroughly informed visitor, Hixon says, "I drove back out the five miles to the middle of nowhere. This big white prison building was surrounded by a 12-foot high fence with razor barbed wire wrapped from top to bottom. In front of the prison were three tall guard towers. I parked in the visitor's section of the parking lot, and made sure my car was locked as I laughed and told myself that 'I don't know why I'm worried about someone stealing my car and personal belongings. Hell, all the criminals are all locked up inside!'"

As Hixon started towards the penitentiary, he "was met by a guard who greeted and escorted me through the large steel doors of the main building entrance." Though he knew it had to be safe, still he "had an insecure feeling once inside and once those steel doors shut behind me. I suddenly realized I was inside a maximum security prison and around some of the world's most dangerous criminals! I felt trapped!" He'd soon find out that was quite a normal feeling, and with the reassurance of the guard next to him, Hixon took a deep breath, swallowed hard, and continued onward on the surreal journey from mortgage loan lender to Hollywood actor! The transformation was no less than Burt Reynolds had made when he won a middle school footrace and went from loser to class hero.

Next thing, Donnie said he was "taken into an office, where I produced identification, was given instructions, and had my picture taken for the Paramount Pictures I.D. card that was issued to me. It was secured on a string, and had to be worn around my neck at all times when entering and leaving inside the prison. This is when I truly believed this movie business was for real. I still have that I.D. today." At the conclusion of the check-in Hixon was "escorted by a guard out the back of the building and into the 'Big Yard' where I saw a lot of prisoners standing and walking around. As we were walking, I asked the guard how dangerous these guys were." The guard responded, "Whatever you do, don't wander off close to them by yourself, as most in here are violent criminals who would slit your throat, and think nothing about it." That put things in perspective for Donnie in an instant. This was the job he signed on for and yes, the potential for danger was real, and around every corner.

After a short walk, Hixon recalls that he entered the football staging area "through a chain-link fence guarded by armed guards. Then we crossed the football field where *The Longest Yard* would be filmed" onward "to a large warehouse that had a truck loading dock across the front." In addition to providing a football field with fresh turf inside a fenced off area in back of the main prison building, they also provided for a warehouse full of "prison uniforms, football uniforms, plus anything and everything that might have been or could be used in filming of the movie." Donnie also took note that all the football equipment was set up like a locker room. "After showing me the warehouse, the guard led me back through the football field, back across the prison yards, through and out the main building." Day one at Georgia's maximum security prison was nearly done.

But not before he got a quick taste of what being the stand-in double for the world's top actor might include. "As I was getting into my car, some college girls from Georgia Southern pulled into the visitor's parking lot and asked me where Burt was. Of course, I had no answer for that... When they asked me if I was from Hollywood, and what role was I playing I told them, 'No I was not from Hollywood, and I informed them I was going to be Burt's stand-in. That really got their attention!'" According to Hixon, "Then they got real excited and friendly, and got out the car and each gave me a big hug before they left. I was starting to like the idea of being in the movie already, especially as Burt's stand-in. Little did I know that day, but that attention would only escalate, all because of being associated with a man named Burt Reynolds, whom I hadn't been introduced to yet!"

With his ego bolstered quite a bit, Hixon headed 15 miles southeast from Reidsville to the equally small town of Glennville, where motel reservations had been made for all the actors and former NFL stars taking part in the movie. Hixon's was one of a number of such motels and trailer camps that surrounded the Route 301 interchange, popular in the day with tourists making their ways to and from Florida and the Georgia coast. Glennville is home to Smith State Prison, one of several state penitentiaries in the region. Hixon notes that, "There was a restaurant in the middle of all the motels and campers that stayed open 24 hours for travelers." Surprised tourists, notable actors, former football stars, penitentiary workers — and prisoners too — at Reidsville, all rubbed shoulders during those more than two months that Hollywood came to south Georgia in the fall of 1973.

You needed to rise and shine early each morning, recalls Hixon, if you wanted to "eat breakfast at the restaurant, drink coffee, or shoot the breeze before boarding the buses" for Reidsville State Prison. Two Trailways buses with the same drivers were hired to "pick up the movie crew and football players before daybreak every morning to take us to the prison. We got to know them by name. After a long day of filming, wrap time was announced and the buses would be parked outside the prison to take us back to the motels. They were always punctual." Then came the part that Donnie enjoyed most. "You could always count on spectators waiting outside on the highway in front of the prison watching us board the buses. And a lot of fans blowing their car horns and waving at the buses on our way back."

According to Hixon, once the cast and crew arrived back at the hotels, "...cars would pass by... all hoping to catch a glimpse of Burt Reynolds."

No chance of that happening in Glennville, though, as Reynolds occupied a house on prison grounds back at Reidsville. "To be a part of something this big was fast becoming very exciting for me!" recalls Hixon. Once back at the motel, "Some would eat an evening meal at the all-day, all-night restaurant in Glennville, while others would converge in large groups and drive to the nearest steakhouse. There you could enjoy a delicious salad, potato, and steak meal. Those south Georgia T-bone steaks were huge..." Plus, says Hixon, "they always had great homemade desserts. The local people in these country towns enjoyed good eating — country style!"

Though Hixon had taken a slightly different career path to Reidsville, Georgia, he made the transition almost seamlessly. "It's strange how different roads in life take you to different destinations," Hixon said. "You just never know what tomorrow will bring, good or bad! This time it was good!" Against all odds, Hixon says "I went from running a loan office and selling investment certificates to shooting a film involving movie stars, producers, directors, and NFL football legends whom I had never met before, and had nothing in common with!" Outside of a few early hiccups, it would not take long for Hixon to mix in with the cast of actors and athletes assembled for the film and to feel somewhat at ease at Reidsville Prison.

"The next morning I boarded the bus with other cast members, and off to the prison we rode," says Hixon. "Once there, we entered through the prison entrance with our ID cards around our neck, exited out the back, and walked through the prison Big Yard." Then, Hixon remembers, "we made our way across the way and entered inside the gates to the football field. This time we were welcomed by two guards armed with shotguns at the gate entrance. I was beginning to feel a little safer. I noticed a lot more important people involved in the movie had arrived, and there were camera crews out on the field. All inside the gate I could hear a lot of enthusiasm in their conversations while they were standing and walking around the football field." The premise of *The Longest Yard* is a football game between the Guard's and the team of inmates known as the Mean Machine. Burt Reynolds' character Paul "Wrecking" Crewe. Crewe quarterbacked the Mean Machine and had been a former professional player kicked out of the league in a point shaving scheme.

Hixon was filled with excitement and ready to meet some of these people that would be in the movie. "This old guy, *I mean he was old-looking,* dressed in his prison uniform wearing a hat approached me and reached out for a handshake saying, 'Hi, I'm John "Pop" Steadman, everybody calls me Pop.' I introduced myself and told Pop I was from Augusta, Georgia, and pleased to meet you." And then, *the almost seamless transition part.* "After shaking hands I asked," says Hixon, "Say, how long have you been in this jail?" The old man answered back, "like I should know who he was, and with a loud, angry tone in his voice, 'I'm no damn prisoner, *I'm an actor from Hollywood!'"*

"After accepting my apology," Donnie said "Pop told me about movies he previously was in, and we got along good after that, as he turned out to be a super person. Three years later, we would meet again on location in Savannah, Georgia, during the filming of the Universal Pictures movie, *Gator,* in which he plays the part of Burt's Dad." Another actor Donnie met was 7'4" giant actor Richard Kiel. "This guy was huge, but was gentle as a kitten. After *The Longest Yard,* Kiel had a big part in a James Bond movie, plus many others. I and other the cast members had a lot of fun kidding around with Kiel during the filming of *The Longest Yard.*"

You would have thought that Donnie would have learned from the Pop Steadman gaffe not to try and read the book by its cover his first go around with the cast and crew. But no, "Hollywood" Hixon was content to learn things the hard way. "I stuck my foot in my mouth again when I met co-producer, Alan Horowitz," recalls Hixon, "whom I mistakenly thought was the prison warden... He was very nice, a handsome man with grey hair, and he definitely looked the part of being important, distinguished, and wealthy." Donnie leaned in as Horowitz related how Reidsville came to be *The Longest Yard*'s film location. Speaking with "one of the prison guards and others who gathered about," the movie producer told of a facility in the southwest "where the prisoners rioted and set fire to the prison."

The Longest Yard's path to Georgia was a journey of its own. The film had originally been scheduled for production at the Oklahoma State Prison at McAlester, Oklahoma. Complete with a football field, the facility known as "Big Mac" seemed a natural for the movie. But plans took a dramatic turn on July 27, 1973, when one of the worst penitentiary riots in United States history broke out at the prison. Three inmates lost their lives, 21 officials were taken hostage, and the prison was set afire in the three-day standoff. Damages totaled in excess of 20 million dollars.

In the wake of the disaster, producer Albert S. Ruddy scrambled to find another facility in short order to host the Paramount Pictures release. A window of opportunity opened to the state of Georgia. Reynolds' breakout role in Deliverance had been filmed along the Chattooga River in North Georgia in 1971, and with it, one million dollars flowed into the local economy. With eyes wide open, then-Governor Jimmy Carter made it no secret that Georgia was serious about the filmmaking industry.

Despite obvious concerns, the Georgia Department of Corrections was persuaded that a movie might make for good morale among inmates, especially if they were allowed to audition for paying roles in the film. The warden at Reidsville State Prison, Joe Hopper, weighed in that there was benefit in a football field at the site. Before long, the state corrections department availed the maximum security facility in South Georgia, with strict adherence that those associated with the film – actors, football players and production staff – be checked daily upon entry and exit. The state's decision to host the movie had a profound impact on 15 members of the Augusta Eagles semipro football team, and two coaches, none more so than Augusta native Donnie Hixon.

Donnie also remembers from the same setting that Horowitz commented, "Burt Reynolds was going to be well liked by all at this prison who meet him!" The public relations machine at Reidsville State Prison kicked into overdrive in an effort that prisoners would grow acquainted with the actor. In his book, *My Life,* Reynolds relates that, "Having shot films in prisons before, I sent down a bunch of movies in which I played a badass and had them screened for the prison population. These guys didn't get the chance to see many of the new movies, but they ran mine every night until we got there. By that time they thought I was okay." From a production standpoint, *The Longest Yard* broke ground in a myriad of ways. Prisoners auditioned for and won small roles in the movie. Paramount Pictures picked up the tab.

The movie company also paid for a fence to ring the newly sodded football field at Reidsville State Prison, to the tune of $100,000, and for additional security to be maintained. In an article written by Henry Woodhead for *The Atlanta Journal Constitution Magazine,* 34-year-old Joe Hopper, Reidsville's warden at the time, related, "There's been a lot of unrest lately. When you get this many people inside a prison, you can't help but be concerned about their welfare. We got together in a meeting with the producer and director and decided that security must come first."

Other frightening topics were also covered that first day on the job. "Later that afternoon," Hixon recalls, "some of the actors and camera people from Hollywood got a bit jumpy when a guard announced there was threat of a severe thunder storm warning on the way that may produce hail and high winds, and possibly a tornado. There were really dark clouds starting to roll across the sky and you could hear lightning strikes in the far distance," remembers Donnie, who waged a lifelong battle with threats of tornados. From the time he was a youngster, pictures of tornado damage he viewed in the local *Augusta Chronicle* the bejesus out of him. Not only was Hixon not fond of twisters, but "Some of those California folks were well aware about all the tornados and mass destruction... and were really scared, and knew that many tornados happened in Georgia... Several said they didn't mind the earthquakes in California," but had no desire to be in a tornado in the Peach State.

"The Hollywood crowd really got scared when someone from Alabama in the crowd told them about a tornado he and his family went through, and described in detail the property damage and lives lost. Hearing that made some of the Hollywood crew even more scared." Though he would never admit it, Hixon, too, was on edge with the subject matter at hand. "This happened right at the end of tornado season," said Hixon, "and after that, I remember we had some rain, but no thunderstorms, as winter was setting in. In the days ahead a few of those California guys would still get a little nervous if the wind started blowing hard, and (were) kidded by some of the Southern boys."

Before the day was out, Burt's makeup man, Guy, came over and informed Donnie that he'd need a haircut for the movie. After he sat down in the chair by the table that had been set up, Donnie was informed by the stylist, "I'm going to cut your long hair a little shorter... that his instructions were to cut Donnie's hair the same style and length as Burt's. Do what you've got to do," Hixon said. "The last time I didn't get a choice on a hair style was that first day in the Marines at Parris Island.

"Filming hadn't started up yet," Hixon relates, and "as the film crews were busy setting up, the cast stood around getting acquainted and acclimated." Donnie could relate more to the athletes in the cast than the actors at that point and the next performers he met were former NFL players Pervis Atkins and Ernie Wheelwright, whom he recognized from their NFL days. Introductions went off without a hitch. "I was very impressed and enjoyed the conversation with them... We enjoyed our first lunch prepared by the catering service that day, and the days ahead, outside on the prison picnic grounds." As he became more comfortable with his surroundings, Hixon settled in nicely with the Hollywood and NFL stars, and was eager to get going, though he still hadn't met Burt Reynolds, the reason he was at Reidsville in the first place.

In his book, *My Life*, Burt Reynolds relates, "The first day of shooting in Reidsville, (Bob) Aldrich (the director of *The Longest Yard*) made a speech to the entire cast and crew. It was the same speech he gave on every picture; it could have been a Marine sergeant on the first day of basic training. One of you is an asshole, he said. I don't know which one, but one of you is. And when you rear your ugly head, I'll chop it off. Good luck, gentlemen." Burt also wrote, "I'm convinced nobody was as hard-nosed and tough a director as Bob Aldrich... I was flattered that he wanted me, battered knees and all." That's where the other #22, Augustan Donnie Hixon enters the picture.

“We
would
hear about
other fights
& stabbings...”

On the Job

Over the next days and weeks, the production settled into a routine, though many things were consistent. Hixon remembers that... "we would arrive on location in the prison yard each morning at daybreak. There we were treated with refreshments such as hot soup, coffee, drinks, snacks, and those Krispy Kreme doughnuts. One morning I saw the giant, Richard Kiel, eat a dozen — he loved them!" It was hardly a breakfast of champions.

Then there was the "large film truck loaded down with many high-powered movie cameras, lighting, and all the other necessary equipment on it." Much of the film equipment, Hixon had never seen before. "Having never been on a movie location before, it was really intriguing, watching the film crew move around in that truck to different locations, get set up, and film. Being there to witness the great acting talent of Burt and the other actors was amazing. They were really good. Whenever they filmed close-ups for speaking parts, they would position bright lights that lit up the actor's faces."

"At daylight, prior to any scene to be filmed, you could count on seeing a man with a sundial type of instrument in his hand. He used it to always keep track of the position of the light and the shadows, and was something I had never seen in use before. It seemed to me that knowing the light situation was always an important factor before the start and during a film scene. When the film crew and the actors were in place you would hear the film director make with the customary 'roll 'em,' and 'action' cues." At the conclusion of each day the director called out, 'it's a wrap,' and it was time to leave and return to the buses, and the motels after a long day. I mean the days were long," recalls Hixon. "It's a fun thing, (making movies), but it's not really an easy thing because of the long hours. I got to be around a lot of professional football players which I never thought I'd be — Joe Kapp, Ray Nitschke, a lot of heroes. And of course, Burt Reynolds..."

And remember the gun-toting, wig-wearing robber who held up Donnie's office and a bank in downtown Augusta prior to *The Longest Yard* taking place? As coincidence would have it, the assailant convicted on the bank heist was given 10 years in prison. Not just any prison, but the Georgia State Prison at Reidsville, Georgia. When Donnie heard the convicted thief was incarcerated at the prison, he requested to pay the inmate a visit. While he was being escorted to the prisoner's lockup, Hixon was asked how he knew the convict. His reply caught the guard off-guard. "I helped him pull off a robbery once," Hixon related, "only he got caught and I didn't." According to Hixon, the look on the guard's face was priceless, before Donnie confessed that he had been kidding. "You had me worried there for a minute," said the guard.

The first time the two met, the assailant was dressed as a woman, and now as an inmate, with his face pressed up close to the cell bars, Hixon had to stand back in order to make the man's face out at all. In an effort to jog the man's memory Hixon asked the prisoner if he remembered him from the Town Finance robbery, and told how he yanked phones from the wall. The prisoner looked at him in silence, likely not to incriminate himself in any way to another robbery. Then Hixon told the tall man peering out from behind the bars of the promise he'd made to tell the police the man they were looking for was short and Chinese. At that, according to Hixon, "He put a big grin on his face." Hixon told the prisoner why he was at Reidsville, and thanked him for not harming anyone during the robbery. The prisoner simply turned and went to the back of the cell. With that, the other #22, Donnie Hixon, made his way back through the prison's walls to resume filming of *The Longest Yard* with Burt Reynolds.

Then there were the realities of actually working inside a maximum security prison. Several incidents of note happened during the two-plus months that Paramount Pictures was on location. One of those involved a lunchroom fight. In the movie, "when Burt (Crewe) solicited the convicts to play against the Guards, he promised them 'no work details and special food,' something they were not accustomed to. The script for *The Longest Yard* called for the Mean Machine to eat a meal that consisted of steak." Since it was raining outside on the day of the intended scene, producers decided to shoot the scene in the prison lunchroom.

"While we were waiting, lined up along the prison hall walls in our prison uniforms to enter," Hixon relates, "a guard came out and prevented the camera crew and us from going in. An actual prison fight had broken out, and a prisoner had been stabbed pretty badly. He was brought out on a stretcher covered in blood, and another was escorted out by two guards in handcuffs. The stabbed prisoner wasn't moving or saying anything, so we didn't know if he was dead or not. After a short wait for them to get the lunch area cleaned up and back in order, they allowed us to go in for the filming where we all enjoyed that steak meal!"

"We would hear about other fights and stabbings while we were there," recalls Hixon. "You didn't know if somebody was going to try and make a hero out of us there... but those guys when you saw them, when they'd work out with us, they looked like they wouldn't harm anybody. But when others told me about some of them, *you wouldn't believe what they did!...* that was kind of scary." Much has changed in America in the nearly half a century since *The Longest Yard* was filmed, and Hixon feels it would be long odds that another movie like it will ever be made. "Today, I doubt many producers would attempt to film a movie like *The Longest Yard* inside the walls of a maximum security prison around killers, drug dealers, and the like. Especially the way the climate, attitude, and violence in the country, and prisons has escalated – too risky and dangerous! Honestly, I wouldn't be too eager to do it again!"

There is also the scene in the movie in which James Hampton's character, "Caretaker," is killed off after a light bulb explosion in his cell. Because a fire was part of the scene, it could not be filmed inside the actual prison. So Hollywood built an exacting set to mimic a cell within the huge warehouse that Paramount utilized to store football equipment, uniforms and other such clothing needed for the production. In real life, the stunt man who actually turned on the exploding light bulb, Frank Orsatti, sustained burns in the scene. Despite the asbestos suit he was wearing, fire found an opening and seeped into the stunt man's gloves. As he frantically signaled for aid, the stunt man was sprayed down with CO_2 canisters, and his suit was torn off. Still he was left with "long and fat blisters" on his hands which, according to the *Atlanta Journal Constitution*'s Woodhead, he "dipped into a plastic pail of water..." The work of a stunt man was serious business!

Meeting Burt Reynolds

"The third day I was there would be the first time I ever saw him (Burt Reynolds) in person," recalls Donnie. "That will always be a special memory I will never forget, seeing him that day walking across the prison Big Yard, through the guarded gate and into the enclosed football field. I heard some prisoners holler out, "Here comes Burt, ya'll. It's really Burt Reynolds." Others yelled out "Hey, Burt, while clapping, whistling, and cheering him on!" When the players and movie people saw him entering inside the gates of the field, you could hear some saying out in loud excited voices "Yonder here he comes everybody, he's here!" His presence was electrifying and changed the mood and morale of everyone there! He brought excitement and electricity to the air, and I was there to see it! A cocky and confident looking Burt went around shaking hands with everybody."

Then came Hixon's turn to meet the man he'd stunt double for in the movie. "The first time I met him, he came up to me, he started walking toward me, and he was chewing gum and shook hands with me, and said 'I'm Burt Reynolds,' like I didn't know who that was," said Hixon. "I shook hands with him and got a shoulder hug," relates

Hixon. "Reynolds had that charisma, charm, and a big smile on his face while chewing gum, and that look and walk about him, which made you know he was somebody special. He was! I have lot of good memories of him, but seeing and meeting him in person that first day was my favorite. This was my first time ever meeting a famous movie star who fast became a legend and a household name around the world." Says Hixon, "He (Burt) was something, I'll tell you that.

"I can see him right now," recalls Donnie. "He was just a special person with a great personality. He never met a stranger. I saw him, and he was no phony, that's why I liked him, he wasn't a phony... If you were ever around Burt Reynolds in person, there's no question why you wouldn't know he was a superstar." And while Hixon is hardly what you would refer to as a shy person, "When I first met him," says Donnie, "I was intimidated, to tell you the truth, I was at a loss sometimes for what to say around him. I had never been around anybody that famous."

Reynolds, at age 37, just over a year removed from the infamous Cosmopolitan magazine photo release was in great shape when *The Longest Yard* was filmed. In his books and interviews about *The Longest Yard*, Reynolds proclaimed that it was he who Ray Nitschke pounded relentlessly during filming. After all, the Hollywood stunt man and leading actor, Burt Reynolds surely wouldn't need someone to take the hits for him, and that is likely how Hollywood might like it recorded. But *Sports Illustrated*'s Edwin Shrake, who wrote an article at the time of the movie's release in September, 1974, knew better. "The usual rule," Shrake wrote, "is that any time an actor is required to leave his feet, or there is any impact, a stunt double is brought in." Or in Donnie Hixon's opinion, any time an actor runs the "risk of getting run over by a freight train like Ray Nitschke, the NFL All-Pro and future Hall of Famer from the Green Bay Packers..."

"Instead, says Hixon, they hire somebody like me who will take the chance of getting their ass busted, and run the risk of a serious injury. Sometimes I think about the football risk I took, not to mention being around dangerous convicts! That was some kind of experience!" Still, Donnie Hixon the stunt double, has always been quick to attest to Burt Reynolds' athleticism. *"Let's make this clear," says Hixon, "he didn't need me or anyone else to stand-in for him. Had they let him, he would have been two times better! He was that good of an athlete. Being his stand-in was an honor,* and like my time spent in the Marines, it would turn out to be another life-changing experience for me."

"After I got in there and I met all of the NFL stars, I thought, why in the world, what in the world am I doing *here*? I was really intimidated around them, especially Burt Reynolds. He was really a great guy... you've got to remember who he was, he was something, he wasn't a phony. And I was really intimidated by him. He had it all. Burt had the looks. I mean, it didn't take me long to figure out, I see why he was a top movie star." Hixon also remembers a conversation with Burt in which Reynolds told Donnie, "...when he finished acting school in New York, he headed back to Hollywood for some unfinished business to become a stunt man – and to accomplish his dream to become a movie star! In talking with him, I could tell he was the type person who had a lot of grit, determination and perseverance, and nothing was going to stop him from achieving his dream!"

During the third week of the filming, WJBF-TV Channel 6 newsman Chris Naylor contacted me one evening and requested to come down and interview Burt. I thought the logical person to ask would be Burt himself. Reynolds said OK, and told me to tell Chris to tell the prison guards out front he was coming to interview him. During lunch break I used a prison office phone, and notified an excited Chris Naylor, who arrived the next morning with his camera man. I remember that day very well and watched him interview Burt. After the interview was over, and Chris was gone, Dave Davies, the publicist for the film, approached me and asked me to 'Step over here, young man.' I knew by his voice tone and look on his face that this wasn't going to be good! That's probably the worst ass-chewing I can ever remember. It reminded me of the ass-chewing's I witnessed from those Marine Drill Instructors during my boot camp training at Parris Island! With insulting and hateful words he let me know I had no authority to invite anyone to arrange interviews with Burt! That was his job! I tried to explain that I asked Burt, but his personality was like those D.I.'s, and would not let me talk. He wouldn't let up! Finally Burt came over and told him that I did ask him, and after hearing it from Burt, he walked off, pissed off! In my opinion, without a doubt, he would have made a hell-raising mean Drill Instructor! He would have been good at it! I didn't take it personal and I understood he was doing his job. He was probably a nice person, but I never found out because I stayed away from him after that."

Hixon fondly recalls that "the following year when the movie was released, a picture of Burt and me was featured on the front page of the Sports Section in *The Augusta Chronicle*. Unbelievable! *See, as they say, 'You never know in life what tomorrow will bring.' I would have never thought this.* When I would come home from filming on our day off, it was not unusual for girls (some I didn't even know) to bring the magazine by for me to take back and get Burt's autograph on that famous *Cosmopolitan* centerfold," says Hixon. "Burt never hesitated to sign, and a couple of times, while smiling, he would ask kiddingly, 'Wait a minute, what does this girl look like?'"

Meeting Dinah Shore

One sunny, crisp fall day in south Georgia, Burt and his adopted brother, Jim (Hooks) Nicholson, (who later went by the name James Hooks Reynolds), were summoned to the opposite end of the football field at Reidsville Prison, away from where filming was taking place. There, two Georgia State troopers stood guard next to Burt's girlfriend at the time, singing and acting legend Dinah Shore, and Reynolds' mom and dad. The cast and crew took advantage of the opportunity to take a break on the manicured green grass that had been put in place for the film. As they were sprawling about, Nicholson returned to the group and informed Donnie that Burt wanted to see him. It was obviously tough being Reynolds' body double, being shown off as such, but someone had to do the job. Hixon took some well deserved ribbing as he got up to leave the crew.

Upon reaching the other end zone, Hixon remembers, "Burt introduced me to his mom and dad, then to Dinah Shore." Burt's parents wanted to see for themselves this so-called stunt double for their son and give him the once over. Burt's father was the police chief in Riviera, Florida, at the time, a chiseled former WWII veteran, and according to Hixon's assessment, "...was a tall, strong, handsome (and) serious-looking man, probably the type you wouldn't want to get on his wrong side. Looking at him, I could tell he was the type of person that meant business if someone crossed him." Of Burt's mom, Hixon said she was pretty "and very nice, and in (his) opinion, where (Burt's) dark hair and good looks came from."

Though Hixon did little talking during the introductions, Dinah Shore noted a familiar twang in Hixon's dialect. "Donnie, where are you from," she asked," you sound like you are from Louisiana." Hixon replied, "No ma'am, I'm from Augusta, Georgia," to which Shore remarked, "I do like your southern-sounding voice." Donnie was immediately smitten with her and described Dinah Shore as hauntingly beautiful. "At that time she was the most beautiful woman I ever met!" said Hixon, and "I admit I was nervous the whole time." Hixon recalled a conversation with Reynolds, in which Burt confided that he fell in love with Dinah after seeing her on television, while attending high school and college. "After seeing her," said Donnie, "I could definitely see why!"

During the film schedule, Hixon had the opportunity to make it real for a longtime friend from Augusta, Don Tyre. "Donnie called me and says, look man, you got to come to Reidsville," said Tyre. "They've got gorgeous women everywhere. I was single and he knew that would intrigue me, and it did. I'll get you down on the field. I'll introduce you to Joe Kapp, Burt Reynolds and all the cast members." Tyre made the hour-and-a half trek south to Reidsville the very next day. "I bounced around on the field like a movie star... I had long hair back then, that was kind of the style back then," he recalls. "I felt like a movie star. It was just a great day in my life."

Meeting Eddie Albert

Decorated war hero Eddie Albert was a grizzled veteran of stage and screen when *The Longest Yard* was filmed in 1973. Albert made his film debut in *Brother Rat* (1938) alongside Ronald Reagan and starred in two "Longest" movies – *The Longest Day* (1962) and *The Longest Yard* (1974). Donnie remembers Albert being on the pensive side, but "When I told him I was an ex-Marine, he opened up some saying he enlisted in the Navy and was a World War II veteran. He made a few comments about the war, but I don't recall him ever mentioning being awarded the Bronze Star for his bravery in the war for rescuing 47 stranded U.S. Marines during a 3-day battle in Tarawa. He also aided in the rescue of 30 more Marines. What a hero!

"Looking at him It was obvious to me he was a physically tough man back in the day, and the above heroic actions mentioned above speak for themselves! His body and mind were in excellent physical and mental condition, as he didn't walk limping around like you would normally see in most 67-year-olds! He was a nice guy, very professional, and obviously highly honorable and respected by the others in the movie... A class act!"

“Don’t try that shit again, Hixon...”

Meeting Mr. Nitschke

Burt Reynolds aside, the actor that Donnie Hixon feared most and would meet face-to-face for the next five weeks of scrimmages was the newly retired NFL star, Ray Nitschke. Like Donnie and Burt Reynolds, Ray worked hard for everything he had in life. Hixon has instant recall of *all things* Nitschke at Reidsville Prison. "The first day I saw him," says Donnie "he and the other guards were dressed in their issued prison guard uniforms – dark blue trousers, navy blue hats (like you see on highway patrol officers), tailored medium blue pilot shirts with buttoned down chest pockets, buttoned down shoulder epaulets that ran through a loop, and buttoned down on the end toward the neck. That uniform really showed off his intimidating physique. He looked scary huge, very muscular. Even though he spoke with very nice manners, you knew of his reputation as a hard-hitting linebacker with the Green Bay Packers. And Nitschke carried that look on his face that could quickly change into 'Man, I can kick your ass.' Therefore you didn't want to make him mad!

"After hearing those stories about what a monster he was on the football field, and seeing him for the first time in person, it was mind-bending," recalls Hixon. "What in the hell have I gotten myself into, he's going to kill me!" The recently retired Nitschke weighed in at a rock-solid 240 pounds. "I weighed only 179 pounds at the time, and that was only after I had eaten a large meal," Hixon says half-jokingly. "I'm thinking a collision with him is comparable to an 18-wheeler hitting a Volkswagen. Not very good odds! No wonder they didn't allow Burt to get hit. Believe me, if given the chance he (Burt) would not have shied away."

The future Hall of Famer got his way with movie producers who were willing to go to extra lengths to appease the NFL standout. In one instance, Donnie recalls, "I was next to Ray when they issued the Guards their football uniforms. Ray was handed the #66 jersey, the same number he wore while playing for the Packers." Likewise, the other former NFL stars would wear the numbers from their playing days in the movie. "But Nitschke refused to accept the jersey, got outraged, and threw it back at the scared equipment person. The assistant director came back later and asked, 'What's the problem Ray?' Ray responded, 'I don't have a problem you've got one, I'm not wearing #66 in the movie!' The producer informed him that Joe Kapp and the other NFL players are wearing their NFL jersey numbers, and none of the others seems to have a problem with it."

Hixon leaned in closely to see how this epic Hollywood versus NFL showdown, of which he had a front row seat, would play out. Just like in his playing days, Nitschke did not back down. "Showing signs of getting angry," relates Hixon, "and looking like he was about to get pissed off, Ray stood up and scolded the assistant director, *'Coach Vince Lombardi put #66 on me, you movie people are not him and didn't play for him, so get the hell out of here before I get mad!'* That producer left out of the locker room in a hurry! They didn't bother him about it anymore, and Ray wore #61, not his Green Bay Packer #66 jersey, in the movie."

Donnie recalls that it didn't matter what jersey number Nitschke wore, it was not something you soon forgot. "The first scrimmage we had was when I really got a good look at him dressed out in a football uniform for the first time. It was intimidating just looking at him! He was the middle linebacker on the Guards' team, wearing the #61 jersey. I'm at quarterback on the Mean Machine, under center, calling signals for the first time in a live scrimmage. This would be my first time playing against the best pro middle linebacker ever. Can you imagine! When we broke the huddle and got up to the line of scrimmage, I looked over the center, face-to-face with Mr. Nitschke, who looked like he was going to kill somebody!"

Though he'd played quarterback for the Augusta Eagles, going up against a future Hall of Famer was a big upgrade in opposition for Donnie, who saw Nitschke as a "beast" when it came time to play football. "While he was yelling out defensive signals, I could see that his front teeth were missing, which made him look even more ferocious inside that large face mask! On that very first play, the offensive right guard apparently got a little nervous when Ray stepped up to the line of scrimmage... and he moved before the ball was hiked. Ray knocked him several yards into the backfield, then ran over him. When we re-huddled, the guard who got knocked on his butt said, 'Damn, Nitschke came to play,' and another said 'Welcome to Ray Nitschke football y'all.'"

Hixon recalls that the first two and a half weeks at Reidsville were days of constant scrimmages. Uniforms that reeked with sweat were never washed in order that they'd be consistent as the production continued. Burt Reynolds and Donnie Hixon both donned #22 jerseys in the film, but it was Hixon who took the ensuing blows in live scrimmages. That of course, meant being tackled hard by Ray Nitschke, who knew only one way to play the game, to the max.

In one instance, Donnie got stomped, literally, by Nitsckhe. "In a live scrimmage," says Hixon, "Mr. Nitschke hit me, drove me back, and knocked me down in the end zone. The hit was bad enough, and I landed face down on my stomach," recalls Donnie. "While attempting to get up, Nitschke got carried away, and stomped me with his big foot in my lower back. I knew this was something you expect to see in a wrestling match on TV, but not in a football game. Did I get mad? No, I was not about to! Would you? The director must have like it, because they showed that play in the movie!"

In another live scrimmage involving a draw play," recalls Hixon, "at the snap of the ball the receivers took off straight down the field, and running backs Joe Jackson and Sonny Sixkiller divided, then sprinted toward the sidelines. That left the middle of the field wide open, and I took off running for a 40-yard gain. The next time I tried that same play, Mr. Nitschke didn't follow the running back and was waiting for me. I had nowhere to go, and as I was running toward him up the middle, I'm thinking a collision with him is not going to be good, so I tried to jump over him. You know who won that battle. He hit me in mid-air, drove me *into* the ground, and landed on top of me! I heard the director say that's a take. Meanwhile, while Ray was lying on top of me looking through that large face mask touching mine, he was smiling with his front teeth missing. What a scary sight! I still remember what he said to me, *'Don't try that shit again, Hixon.'* After he said that, I said 'Yes sir, boss' and got up! When I went back in the huddle, one of the players said to me – 'Man, you got the shit knocked out of you!' My answer was, 'Yeah, tell me about it.'"

Hixon recalls another such play when he tried to go up the middle against the bruising middle linebacker. "...I went back to pass, but instead kept the ball, and ran up the middle. Big mistake once again, as I never made it across the line of scrimmage and was jolted backwards to the ground by Nitschke's hit. This time wasn't as bad," Donnie remembers, "as he didn't land on top of me with his 240 pounds." In his book, *My Life,* Burt Reynolds shared that "...When I stared across the line of scrimmage, there was always one man looking back more intently than any of the others. Nitschke, the Green Bay Packers' old linebacker, was a gentle, lovely man — until he put a football helmet on. Then he thought he was in the Super Bowl." Wrote Reynolds of Nitschke, "He was intent on making every man on the other team cry."

Reynolds, himself a star running back in high school and college, took solace at watching Hixon get pounded by Nitschke and even gave Donnie some useful tips from his own playing days. "I remember Burt telling me to play smart, and when I get tackled by Nitschke, not to resist the impact, not to brace myself and become stiff, but to get my feet off the ground and stay loose!" According to Hixon, Reynolds also imparted, "That's the reason why drunks don't seem to get hurt bad in car wrecks." Donnie says he heeded Burt's advice which "may have prevented me from getting injured. Also, I knew from elementary school football," recalls Donnie, "to avoid falling on the back of my head, and to always try landing on my butt."

"Lets face it," Hixon told *Chronicle Herald* writer Robert Eubanks for a newspaper article in 1974, "I really could have gotten hurt. I was hit real hard a couple of times... we kept rerunning one scripted play because the director said it wasn't realistic enough. Believe me, he (Nitschke) finally made it real."

In his autobiography, *My Life*, Burt Reynolds recalled a scene with Nitschke that called for a few curse words. Mean Machine punter/ kicker "Charlie Blue Eyes," played by Stan Kanavage, was to dropkick the football, to which Nitschke's character, Bodanski, was to ask, "What the hell was that?" Reynolds' character, Paul "Wrecking"

Crewe's scripted reply was, "A drop kick, you stupid son of a bitch." Nitschke would have nothing of the dialogue, on the grounds that his three children would see the film. In his book, Reynolds wrote that he pleaded Nitschke's case to director Bob Aldrich, whose refused to give in, and told Burt to, "Call him a stupid son of a bitch and and run like hell." Exactly what Reynolds says he did on the very next play, only to find that Nitschke "reached out and caught me. Then he squeezed, pulled, and twisted the front of my jersey off. I looked up from the turf, where he'd thrown me, and saw the bottom half of my #22 in his hands – which is the way you see it in the film." Director Bob Aldrich got his shot, Burt got pounded, Nitschke got his way, and for the moment at least, the other #22, Donnie Hixon, did not have to take a pounding.

"One day after I got to know him better," Donnie says of Nitschke, "I saw him take his false teeth out and got up enough nerve to ask him about them. He said it happened during his sophomore year at the University of Illinois while playing Ohio State. He was on the kickoff team, was not wearing a face mask, and took a big hit in the mouth, which caused him to lose his four front teeth. Later after getting false teeth, he said he would always take them out when it came time to practice or play in a game.

"In other conversations, Ray told me he was a quarterback and a safety in high school who liked to fight! He'd say "Man, I loved to fight back then." Hixon says he told Nitschke "he should have stayed with it; he could have been another Rocky Marciano. With that laugh of his, he said no, that he always wanted to be a quarterback and play college football. He said he entered the University of Illinois as a quarterback, but during his sophomore year after coaches saw how aggressive, relentless, and vicious he was on special teams, they switched him to the fullback and middle linebacker positions. Then at Green Bay he was the middle linebacker for legendary coach Vince Lombardi, whom he idolized."

Hixon especially remembers Nitschke's reverence for Lombardi, who led the Packers to their first two Super Bowl wins. "Whenever he talked about Coach Lombardi you could see the emotion in his face and adrenaline start to flow. He gave me the impression that if you said something derogatory about Coach Lombardi, he just might kill you. He loved the man! He said that before a game, Coach Lombardi, in his strong intimidating voice, would tell them 'You've got to play for 60 minutes, no exceptions.' He said the team would be all jacked up when they hit the field." According to Hixon, Nitschke said, "Man, we would let it all hang out, we were always ready, and Coach Lombardi made sure of it." Ray also shared a quote that Lombardi often said to his team, that "Fatigue will make a coward of us all." Hixon recalls that, "Through the years I heard that Lombardi quote many times. When I coached the Augusta Eagles I would bring that quote just before the start of team calisthenics and the running of wind sprints. In talking with Ray, I did learn a few things about his playing days in the NFL, and of Lombardi's coaching techniques that helped me become a better coach in football and a better manager on my job."

As much as Nitschke loved to talk about Vince Lombardi, the NFL players in Reidsville liked to reminisce about their playing days in the NFL against Ray. "Whenever Ray's name was mentioned," recalls Hixon, "Joe Kapp and some of the other pro football players were quick to point out what it was like when other teams prepared to play against the Packers defense. Every time, the players said their offensive coaches would circle Nitschke's name on the drawing board." According to Hixon, "Each coach... would tell their teams that they needed to be able to run the football to be successful on offense, and the only way to win the game was to control Nitschke."

“He had that take-charge, bossy personality...”

Kapp-ing Things Off

Joe Kapp, who engineered the Minnesota Vikings to the Super Bowl in 1970, had an eventful stay in Georgia, both on and off the field during filming of *The Longest Yard.* In early November, Kapp and a member of the movie crew caused a disturbance at a bar in Savannah and were arrested. According to police reports, on Friday night, November 2, 1973, the duo "entered the bar," at the Ramada Inn Lounge on West Boundary Street, "in a loud and boisterous manner." Things escalated and before it was over, a number of charges were lodged against Kapp that included "public drunkenness, fighting, assaulting police officers, and theft of service..." According to the account carried in the *Savannah Morning News* of Sunday, November 4, 1973, Kapp was "released on his own recognizance." The crew member posted $200 bond.

Hixon has fond recollections of a game that Joe Kapp engineered to warm players up after lunch each day. This game that Kapp concocted was a unique combination of several sports, including football, but without the tackling. The point of the game was to advance the ball forward with a series of laterals. In Kapp's game, the ball moved freely until it was either intercepted, fumbled, or knocked from a player's hands. Kapp affectionately named the game, "grab-ass." Hixon recalls, "Fun it was, we played it several times a week, usually when we returned from lunch when we had 20 minutes or so left before filming would start up."

A game named grab-ass worked just fine around NFL players and inmates at Reidsville prison, who had likely heard every name in the book. Nearly a decade later, when Kapp was head coach of the California Golden Bears, he utilized the exact same game as a way for his team to have fun without the major risks of being injured, with one exception. At Cal, he politely referred to the game as "garbazz," which took off the game's rough sounding edges. Different name, same game. "It's Mexican-French for grab-ass, naturally," Kapp was quoted as having said in "The Anatomy of a Miracle," Ron Fimrite's 1973 *Sports Illustrated* article. "We used to play it when I was with the Vikings. It's a mixture of basketball and football with elements of rugby. You just work the ball downfield" by passing it back and forth.

As fate would have it, garbazz, or whatever it was actually called, turned out to be the catalyst for one of the greatest football plays of all-time. You know the play, the one with seconds remaining on the ensuing kickoff in which Cal players lateraled the ball down the field, between and through the Stanford band, for the winning touchdown. It happened in Kapp's first year as head coach of the Bears in 1982. John Elway had just engineered a Stanford drive that ended in a field goal by Mark Harmon, (not of NCIS fame), with four seconds remaining. That put the Cardinal up 20-19 in the regular season finale between the bitter rivals. A penalty for excessive celebrating after the touchdown cost Stanford 15 yards on the spot of the ensuing kickoff. The stars were lining up in Cal's favor. Caught up in the emotion, the Cardinal band prematurely took the field during the kickoff to become the Golden Bears' greatest adversary. Harmon squibbed the kickoff, Cal promptly garbazzed the kickoff downfield. When the Bears' Kevin Moan weaved his way between defenders and the band, and found his way to the Cardinal end-zone, pandemonium ensued.

A stunned crowd of more than 75,000 had witnessed the play live at Memorial Stadium in Berkeley, and countless millions more would view the play on replays from the comfort of their homes over the years. Though the sports world was shocked, Donnie Hixon was not. In fact, Hixon, was hardly surprised at all. "Whenever I first saw that play on television, it brought back memories of Joe teaching us how to play grab-ass on the prison football field during film breaks." Donnie had been part of the same type of play run many times before — albeit without a band's intervention. The play stood, Cal won the game 25-20, and Kapp was named Pac-10 Conference coach of the year. Donnie Hixon shook his head in amazement that it was the old grab-ass play that saved the day for the California Golden Bears and Joe Kapp. Cal finished the season 7-4, the best season in Kapp's five-year reign at Cal.

"...Joe played Walking Boss in the film, and was also a player-coach in the movie." Hixon said, "he was the one in charge of drawing up the offensive plays, the practice and organization of the teams, and coached both offensive teams in scrimmages." Kapp was also instrumental "in any rehearsed plays that involved an actor" in *The Longest Yard*. Hixon relates that after seeing Kapp "play during the NFL season and in the Super Bowl (1970), this was an exciting time for me three years later, actually being coached by him in a movie. It was an honor, as I did learn from that experience, and made use of it when I became head coach of the Augusta Eagles two seasons later! Watching and listening to him was easy to see why a team would rally around him. Joe was a true catalyst. Why was he cast in the movie as The Walking Boss! He had that take-charge, bossy personality about him. He was a tough guy!"

One time, "Someone had challenged Kapp, saying he couldn't drink 12 shots of tequila," recalls Hixon. Afterwards, he was riding with former NFL standout Mike Henry (of Tarzan fame), hanging out the passenger window in downtown Reidsville, shouting profanity. The police chief followed them back to the motel in Glennville, where both got out of their respective cars. According to Donnie, "Joe appeared drunk and having problems standing up. When the chief went to confront him, Joe fell down and commenced throwing up all over the ground." Joe was taken to his motel room, "and the chief left because... he knew who Joe was, and was only going to warn him." Donnie says, "Most coaches, players, and fans would agree that Joe has got to be the toughest to ever play the quarterback position in the NFL.

"The first week I was there," (Reidsville prison), Donnie remembers, "Joe kept calling me 'Chuck.' He thought I was Chuck Hixson," whose last name was spelled differently and had been the standout quarterback in recent years at Southern Methodist University. The scrimmages at Reidsville were high-spirited and rife for bumps and bruises. While on the Guards team during a scrimmage, Joe Kapp was injured by an Augusta Eagles semi-pro player and had to be replaced in the football scenes with a stand-in. Hixon again pulled Burt Reynolds aside and suggested he be replaced with Harlem, Georgia, product Bobby Meybohm. Burt listened to Hixon's advice. "I got on the phone and called my friend in Augusta... At the time he was an excellent all-around strong athlete," relates Hixon. Meybohm made a name for himself in Augusta-area sports circles as a standout athlete at Harlem High School, and later quarterbacked the Augusta Eagles' first full-season team in 1969. "Bobby was a real-estate agent for his brother E.G.'s company," says Hixon. "He was probably only maybe an inch shorter than Joe. He did a good job filling in for the famous Joe Kapp." Upon reporting to Reidsville, Meybohm, a newlywed, donned the #11 jersey for the Guard's team. Kapp retained his duties in running the offenses for the Guards and the Mean Machine.

"...fast
&
reckless..."

Prison Escape

During the second month of filming there was an actual escape from Reidsville Prison. With so much focus on a tiny part of the prison grounds, four inmates hatched a plan of "sweet deception" to break out of the facility. It was the way they tried to escape that was unique. According to *The Atlanta Constitution* of Tuesday, November 9, 1973, the convicts hid in a "vat of sugar cane juice" atop a tractor-trailer headed for the prison's cane mill, located some two miles from the fenced-in grounds where the movie was being filmed. En route to the mill, the four climbed out of the vat and overtook a trustee driving the tractor. Two of the four convicts were picked up on prison land and their clothes reeked of the cane juice. Two convicts were still at large when the newspaper went to print. It already made for a compelling story if it ended there — but of course it didn't.

After a half-day of filming on Saturdays, the cast and crew of *The Longest Yard* were typically free to go their way until the following Monday morning. On occasion, Augusta Eagles running back Joe Jackson would catch a ride back to Augusta with lineman Steve Hood in his shiny, black 1957 Chevy Impala. Hood played fast and reckless on the football field and lived the same way. Donnie referred to Hood as "a hell raiser" and on one particular trip it would catch up with the rugged lineman, and also with running back Joe Jackson, by association. In an attempt to make good time getting home, Hood ran a red light as they entered the city limits of Waynesboro, Georgia, a half-hour south of Augusta. The Impala he was driving was promptly pulled over and a second patrol car followed immediately behind. Unfortunately, both players had left their drivers licenses back at the hotel near Reidsville, and the tag on Hood's car was registered to his work truck. Red flags were flying!

The search for the two escapees from Reidsville State Prison was still ongoing and top of mind throughout the Southeast, as the officers ordered the men outside Hood's Impala. A thorough search of the vehicle turned up a pair of prison uniforms which Hood had thrown in the truck of the car after a day's work on *The Longest Yard.* Hood and Jackson tried to convince the officers that they were part of the cast of the movie being filmed at Reidsville. *Sure, sure, we believe you,* the officers surely thought, *you're part of a movie production about convicts – please turn around now while we put handcuffs on you!* With that, Steve Hood and Joe Jackson, Burt Reynolds' favorite player on the Mean Machine, were promptly driven to the lockdown in Waynesboro, Georgia for safekeeping.

Once inside the jailhouse, the prisoners were told to empty their pockets. Hood and Jackson had just gotten paid and officers watched as each pulled out wads of cash. According to Hixon, the deputies asked the men over and again, "Who you boys robbed?" A phone call was placed to Reidsville State Prison and the prison responded that they'd be back in touch after a head count of inmates was tabulated – and that the process might take two hours. In the meantime, the sheriff knew a resident, a Mr. Tinley, who was familiar with many of the Augusta Eagles, as the man's nephew, Lawton Tinley, played for the semipro team. When the sheriff returned to the jail with said Mr. Tinley an hour and a half later, an exasperated Hood and Jackson called out to the man that he certainly knew them. But with football helmets on most of the time, could anyone be really sure. Mr. Tinley got close up, looked intently at each player, and informed the sheriff that he could not identify them. With that, the sheriff ordered the men to be locked up and left the room as Hood and Jackson demanded to see their lawyers.

The sheriff had known better all along. The jail in Waynesboro had been notified by Reidsville State Prison that all were accounted for – Mr. Tinley and the sheriff had played a ruse on the players. After 15 minutes of a good laugh between the two officers, the sheriff ordered that the the prisoners be released. In the sheriff's office, the entire group had another good laugh before Hood and Jackson got back on the road. Before they did, the sheriff turned to address Hood. In a serious tone, the sheriff warned Hood to get his act together – to always keep his drivers license on his person, not to speed or run red lights, and to get the right license tags on the vehicles he owned. *And while we're at it, those prison uniforms – they need to stay at Reidsville Prison!* Back on the movie set the following Monday, Burt Reynolds and the entire cast and crew of *The Longest Yard* had the last laugh when the antics that transpired over the weekend leaked out. And as best Donnie can recollect, it seems the two prisoners who escaped from Reidsville Prison were still on the lam when production for *The Longest Yard* was complete.

"...that fast-acting gum was the way to go..."

Prison Pranksters

Putting up 100 or so actors, football players, and crew members, the overwhelming majority of whom were male, for over two months in a small town, proved a breeding grounds for pranksters – and sometimes a headache for Paramount Pictures. Number 22 Donnie Hixon relates the best of the best pranks and hijinks during filming of The Longest Yard *at Reidsville Prison in the fall of 1973.*

Chewing Gum Change "It was during that time that Feen-A-Mint laxative also came in the form of gum, and was made to taste like chewing gum. One of the crew members purchased a box of chewing gum from the local drug store, the one that turned your tongue green, along with a box of laxative gum. Then he switched the product inside each of the boxes. About an hour before going outside the prison to the picnic tables for lunch the prankster gave me, Joe Kapp, and others a piece or two which we all stuck in our mouth and began chewing, thinking all along it was chewing gum. While eating lunch that day our stomachs began to growl in a bad way. There were two outside restroom stalls outside the prison walls where we ate, and both happened to be occupied. I remember Joe Kapp beating on the doors hollering 'How much longer, how much longer?' Finally, we couldn't wait any longer and Kapp and I took off running through the main building area, then out through the prison yards to the football bleaches where there was another restroom. Just in time! I can say one thing back then, if you got constipated, that fast-acting gum was the way to go. It did work!"

Halloween Hijinks "I had just cut the television and lights off, and was about to slip into bed one evening, when all of a sudden someone started banging on the motel door. All the while, they yelled repeatedly, 'Hixon, Hixon, get up, you've got an emergency call at the front desk! Hurry, hurry.' I panicked and cut the lights back on, reached for my pants, and while trying to get them on I tripped, and fell backwards, hard on my butt. My mind raced and I hoped nothing happened to a family member. While fumbling with my pants I opened the door only to have the shit scared out of me! There was this Frankenstein-looking creature at the door who let out a big scream and hollered, 'Monster Man' as he lunged toward me. As I tried to get away, I tripped and fell backwards on the floor and landed on my butt again. Then I heard laughing from out in the parking lot and I knew I had been had! One of the film crew members wore one of those skin tight Halloween masks and dressed in an outfit that would have made Count Dracula look bad! After that, I got my shoes and shirt on, and followed along with the others to witness who was next!"

Richard 'Dick' Kiel happened to be next. Just before the creature had a chance to knock, Dick opened the door quickly, shoved the guy backwards, and then slammed it shut hard. Everybody came out from behind the cars, laughing at the crew member creature down on the pavement. Then Dick Kiel opened the door back up, stuck his head out, smiled, and said he heard the commotion from my prank, and was prepared when they came to his door.

Augustan Joe Jack Jackson was next in line to be pranked. We all hid in back of the cars parked in front of the rooms. This time the crew member did the routine a little differently, as he knocked on the door as you normally would. Joe hollered out 'Who is it?' a couple of times, and when no one answered back, he pulled the curtain window back next to the door and peeked out. When he did, the crew member stuck his head against the window pane. When Joe saw him, he let out a yell, 'Get away from here you monster-looking man,' and jerked the curtain down as he ran to the back of the room in panic, desperately trying to find a way to escape! The crew member stayed in front of the window waving his arms up and down saying 'I'm going to get you,' and Joe kept hollering back at him to 'Get away from here you crazy looking thing, go away!' Finally we came out from behind the cars laughing, and through the window, Joe recognized it was us. Then he came out laughing with us. Joe, my friend, was a good sport about it. I told him not to feel bad, that the crew also got me!

"There was a lot of idle time during the filming especially between speaking scenes. Because we had to get up so early each morning, and because some stayed out or up late, many not involved in the scene would lay down to catch a quick nap. Someone was always quick to set a cup of water on them and tickle their noses, which caused them to move, and knocked the water over on themselves! You've got to remember, cold water didn't feel good on a day when it was cold and windy. On several days the temperature in Reidsville dropped to freezing in the early morning."

Ed Blackwell "Ed was an Augusta Eagles player on the Guards team who was particularly good at pulling pranks. In fact, Ed was what I would call a master prankster. We all suspected him in the laxative chewing gum prank, though he would never own up to it. Blackwell honed his pranks to a science and pulled one particular prank at least five times that I remember. The first time he pulled it off was one morning as a crowd stood along the sidelines, then again that afternoon when players were bunched on the ground taking a nap, and another time later that day when the bus took us back to the motels in Glennville. Then for a second straight day he pulled it off a couple more times.

Sulphur dioxide is a colorless gas or liquid that has a strong, choking odor. Blackwell had a small bottle of it, which was in a small dropper bottle that he could squeeze out a drop at a time. Whenever he was in a crowd or boarding the bus, he would inconspicuously drop a few drops around. The smell consumed a large area after only a few drops, therefore it was hard to pinpoint the exact area it came from. When this happened, those around it dispersed immediately, laughing. This stuff was powerful and smelled like rotten eggs. Whenever this happened, you would hear comments like 'That son of a bitch must be rotten inside' or, 'Whoever it is must have shit in his britches,' or 'That's the worst fart I ever smelled,' and the like. Then we had a lot of fun accusing one another who the prankster was, saying things like, 'I know it's you, man, come on, 'fess up.' That was an awful smell. After those two days it didn't happen anymore as Ed's small bottle of sulphur dioxide was empty. Thank goodness! Funny times!"

Pile on "During the last week of the filming, I was chased and taken down in the middle of the field from behind, and did I ever get piled up on. I was getting crushed, and could hardly breathe, all the while thinking I was going die with all that weight on top of me. I tried to stay calm and not panic, and thought if they didn't get off me soon I would be crushed. Whenever I watch a football game now, I know how a player in the NFL and college level feels on the bottom of a pile up! I was never so glad when I was able to get up, feeling relieved to find out I had no broken bones. That was scary, and I've never forgotten that crushing feeling."

Snake in the Grass "My favorite scene in the movie was when they filmed Burt in the fight scene in the muddy swamp for the film. It was there that Bob Tessier (Connie Shockner) captured a large, poisonous cottonmouth water moccasin. Tessier wanted to keep the snake and carry it back to California where there were none. He took the snake back to the prison warehouse, where the locker facility was located, and put it in a large wooden barrel. That afternoon, while most of us were out on the loading dock and waiting to leave for the day, Tessier removed the snake from the barrel and transferred it to a croker sack. Some of the Mean Machine's 300-pound linemen, George Jones (Big George), Steve Wilder (JJ), and Wilbur Gillian (Big Wilbur) just happened to be on their backs on the warehouse's loading dock, taking a well-deserved nap. Lying next to each other, side-by-side, with their feet hanging over the side of the dock, they provided an easy target for someone of Tessier's cunning. Tessier stood over their heads, then pulled the snake out, and said 'Look what I got!' The three big linemen simultaneously woke up, took one look at that snake being held over their faces, jumped off the dock, and ran about a 100 yards onto the football field before ever stopping to look back!

"We all stood there laughing, but the film's associate director didn't think it was so funny. He came over and started chewing Bob out, saying, 'If you had dropped that snake, and it happened to bite one of them, we would be in deep shit. Bob told the director to 'Shut up!' Then he kneeled down and laid the snake down in front of him and bumped it with his fist. The snake curled up and struck him on his hand. 'See it didn't hurt,' Bob said. Tessier teased the snake a second time and let it strike him again!" Donnie recalls that the associate director was cursing and hollering, "You've gone crazy, you fool, that snake is poisonous! Most of us on the deck had cleared out of the way by that point, and when Tessier let it strike him strike him again, someone hollered out 'Man, he's gone nuts!' Laughing, Bob grabbed the snake in back of its head, got up and put it back in the croker sack, all the while getting chewed out by the director.

"What the director and most of us in the cast didn't know, was that Bob had used sutures and put a stitch (just one) in the front of the snake's mouth, which prevented it from actually opening when it struck. Scary! After he had his fun, Tessier took the stitch out, put the snake back in the sack, carried it out of the prison, and put it in a cage inside his trailer."

"Joe Jack"

In short order, Donnie Hixon not only gained the hard-earned respect of Reynolds, Nitschke and the cast of *The Longest Yard* but also had input when players were injured during the movie's brutal football production stage. When a running back went down early in the filming, Hixon pulled Burt Reynolds aside and informed the movie star that he knew of another player from the Augusta Eagles that would be an even better fit for the part. "If he's that good, well, let's get him down here," was Burt's reply. Hixon's own reputation was on the line. He'd bragged how good his friend from Augusta was, now it was time to put up or shut up.

Jackson had been an outstanding high school player at Lucy Laney High School in Augusta, where he excelled as a feared running back on offense and as a bruising linebacker and defensive back. Jackson was coached by legendary and highly respected coach David Dupree, who sent many others off to college, including a number who did very well in the NFL. One such player, says Donnie, was "Joe's hero, Super Bowl III running back Emerson Boozer. Joe came along later and was just as good in high school — even wore Emerson's number — and went to Maryland State on a scholarship as Boozer had. Jackson was feared by all who competed against him... but unlike Emerson, he fell through the cracks and didn't get through the first year in college." According to Hixon, "He came back to Georgia and came out for the Augusta Eagles where I had just begun my first year coaching as the offensive coach.

"Joe made his presence felt right away as a defensive back in his first scrimmage. He was a quick learner and the first time he touched the ball on offense it was quite obvious that he was something special. Very aggressive, strong, and quick as a cat! Joe could deliver a devastating head butt, which was legal back then, and a nasty forearm. In his first game as a running back against the Savannah Indians, he sent four opposing players to the locker room. You could say, he played with bad intentions, just like Ray Nitschke."

Jackson hadn't initially been picked by the Paramount Pictures recruiters who scouted the Augusta Eagles, because a stable of running backs they felt would complement Burt Reynolds in the backfield had already been assembled. But injuries in rough and tumble sports like football are a big part of the game. Especially so in *The Longest Yard*, where director Bob Aldrich had a keen eye for action that was realistic and strived for that endpoint. Hence, the two and a half weeks of live action scrimmages — nearly enough for a full season's worth of hits in a concentrated amount of time — were fraught with injuries. Donnie made a phone call back to Augusta, and in a moment's notice, Jackson was on his way to Reidsville.

When Jackson arrived on location the next day, Burt Reynolds was spellbound by the running back's athleticism. That's quite a statement in itself, since Reynolds, too, was a freight train style running back when he got the ball in high school, and during his injury-prone years at Florida State. Jackson was not only strong, fast and fearless, but despite his diminutive size at 185 pounds, he did something no one else dared — go at Ray Nitschke head-on. On the very first play of his first day at Reidsville, Jackson lined up in the backfield with Hixon at quarterback. According to Hixon, "Jackson was chomping at the bit to play against Nitschke."

Just before Hixon could call the play, players were told to hold up so an adjustment to a camera could be made, an ongoing, but necessary part of film production. "All the while," says Donnie, "Jackson couldn't wait to get his hands on the football." When production resumed, Hixon "called Jackson's number on toss to the left. But instead of going wide as scripted, Jackson cut back inside for a head-on collision with Nitschke. The NFL great knocked him five yards back in the air." Despite the collision, says Hixon, "The ultra-talented Jackson simply landed on his feet and hand, popped back up and kept running 40 yards for a touchdown." On the sidelines, Burt Reynolds smiled. Jackson was just as good as Hixon had said he was, maybe even better.

"You could've probably heard that lick outside the prison walls, says Donnie. "That hit by Nitschke would have been lights out for most." The play was so good, Hixon wonders why it wasn't included in the film. He and Jackson would talk about it for years to come when they reminisced about their roles in *The Longest Yard,* usually over a late-night phone call after the movie had aired. "Some found it hard to believe Jackson took that hit" from one of the NFL's best all-time linebackers, "and lived to tell about it." According to Hixon, "Even Ray Nitschke looked surprised. That was just who Joe Jack was... Joe always came to play his best, to get respect from the other team players, as he would say. He was one tough hombre!"

Burt Reynolds was so impressed, he even gave the talented running back from Augusta the nickname, "Joe Jack," quite a compliment coming from the former Florida State standout and certain NFL player had it not been for injuries. Hixon is quick to point out that the 180-pound Jackson was the best player to take part in the film, and "pound for pound the best running back I've ever seen." Hixon has no doubt that Burt would concur. At the end of the production, Hixon looked on as Reynolds personally signed a picture for Jackson, "Go Get Em 'Joe Jack,' You're the best, Your friend, Burt Reynolds, '*The Longest Yard*.'" Of all the players that took part in the production, "In my opinion," Hixon attests, "that was Burt's way of saying Joe was the Most Valuable Player, the best! Joe's face can be seen a lot in the game, the huddles, and on the sidelines. To me that picture Burt signed was an MVP trophy."

According to Hixon, Reynolds even tried to persuade Jackson to go to college at Florida State, and Joe Kapp tried to get the talented Augustan to try the Canadian Football League. But Jackson, who fought demons associated with alcohol, never advanced his football career. Still, he relished taking part in the movie and was forever grateful that his good friend Donnie Hixon had gotten him a part in the film. Jackson may not have made it to the NFL, but he proved his worth to those who saw him perform in *The Longest Yard*. Number 29, Joe Jack, had his moment in the sun.

Reynolds also received an MVP trophy of sorts in the form of a picture from Ray Nitschke. In *My Life*, Reynolds confided, "...what I treasured most, besides the friendships I made, was a picture Nitschke signed for me. He said, 'To a tough son of a bitch.' It was like Cary Grant saying you had class," wrote Reynolds. "I wouldn't trade that for anything." Nitschke also gave Hixon a gift that keeps on giving, though not a picture, unless x-rays count. Hixon's gift came in the form of a mangled finger that today functions with the aid of a titanium rod. Donnie also injured a knee courtesy of a ferocious hit by Nitschke. The pain in the joint grew progressively worse and required surgery several years later. Still, Hixon wouldn't change a thing. Despite the injuries, the experience of testing himself against one of the best linebackers in NFL history and his ongoing acquaintance with Burt Reynolds made it all worthwhile.

Hixon had spent nine weeks in Reidsville in the fall of 1973, and like his time in the Marines, it was a life-changing experience. He returned to his hometown of Augusta, Georgia where Donnie resumed life as it was prior to *The Longest Yard.* For a small town boy who faced tremendous adversity throughout his young life, he had overcome all the odds. Now retired, Donnie Hixon realizes even more the true blessings of his life - a loving family, good health and friends, and memories of a lifetime.

"When filming was over," says Hixon, Paramount Pictures authorized the Augusta Eagles to take possession of the Mean Machine uniforms, helmets, and equipment. The following season the semi-pro team from Augusta took on the nickname of the Mean Machine!" That season of 1974, when *The Longest Yard* hit the big screen, "there were a lot of talented new players who wanted to play for the Augusta Eagles," suddenly the most popular semi-pro team in America. They played like their counterparts in the movie as well, and made their way to a repeat appearance in the Dixie Football League championship game. It would be a rematch of the previous year's title game, against the Greenville Bulls. Says Hixon, "The Eagles players who were back from the '73 game were chomping at the bits to get another shot at Greenville, this time on the Richmond Academy High School football field in Augusta. The Eagles players all dressed out in the same Mean Machine uniforms used in the movie." Burt Reynolds' favorite player in *The Longest Yard,* Joe Jackson, went on a 52-yard touchdown run, and from that point on, Hixon says, "it was all over for the Greenville Bulls."

"...it was a once in a lifetime thing..."

Eagles Soar on Silver Screen

In 1974, members of the Augusta Eagles football team got to see for themselves the roles they played in *The Longest Yard*. Team owner, Dr. Gus Carlucci, the owner of the Eagles, played a doctor and had several speaking lines in the movie. Carlucci also filled a void for Paramount Pictures as an in-house doctor that could attend to on-field scrapes and injuries that happened during filming. The Eagles offensive coordinator and onetime quarterback, #22 Donnie Hixon appeared as Burt Reynolds' stunt double on the Mean Machine. Augusta running back, #29 Joe Jackson also played a starring role for the Mean Machine. Two other members of the Eagles played prominent roles on the Guards team – running back #33 Tony Reese and #11 Bobby Meybohm, the stand-in for injured NFL great Joe Kapp.

On the games opening kickoff, Guards return man, Reese, runs the football back for a touchdown. On the Mean Machine's first play from scrimmage, the Guards' Bogdanski character, played by NFL great Ray Nitschke, scores a touchback. Those two points came at the expense of a tackle in the end zone on #22 Donnie Hixon, and adding insult to injury, Bogdanski stomped on the stunt-double's back.

In a pivotal second quarter scene, #33 Reese takes a handoff and is clotheslined to the ground by the Mean Machine's Samson. Played by actor Dick Kiel, Samson responds, "I think I broke his f****** neck." Dr. Carlucci evokes a similar remark. Late in the game, when the Mean Machine mounts a comeback, #22 Donnie Hixon's running and passing skills and #29 Joe Jackson's running are at centerstage on the big screen.

Other members of the Augusta Eagles played less prominent, but equally important roles in the movie. Eagles' defensive coach, Tom Goforth was a teacher in New Ellenton, South Carolina at the time of the production. Goforth was quoted in an article for The Augusta Chronicle by Robert Eubanks, "Our people were great about it. Yes, our people understood it was a once in a lifetime thing." That being the case, Goforth also utilized the opportunity to record the local history. He deserves major credit as the majority of the photographs from Reidsville in the fall of 1973 that appear in this book were taken by Goforth and later given to his good friend, Donnie Hixon.

Another educator to take part in the production, Eddie Watkins was the principal at Merriweather Elementary School in North Augusta, South Carolina. Watkins played a defensive tackle in the movie, the same position he played in semi-pro football. "I put a lot of miles on the road and never did miss more than three days at a time," Watkins told Eubanks. "I was in an unusual position as school administrator. Everyone wanted to know about the movie and Burt Reynolds, of course. They can ask you thousand questions about it."

An Eagles defensive tackle, Howard Silverstein played the center position on the Guard's team and after *The Longest Yard*, was signed to a tryout with the Birmingham Americans of the World Football League. A helicopter pilot in Vietnam, Ed Ramon played center for the Augusta Eagles, and switched to defensive line for *The Longest Yard.*

More Eagles in *The Longest Yard*

Ben "Sarge" Johnson, *Mean Machine Special Teams,* and *Guards team players* **Jim Bates, Ed Blackwell, Steve Hood, Terry James, Larry James, David Mathis, Bill Rampley, Ken Satterlee.**

Of special note, during scouting of The Augusta Eagles, Paramount Pictures overlooked the team's offensive guard, Freddie Perry, who according to Donnie Hixon, "was quick as a cat." Freddie is the older brother of William "Refrigerator" Perry, and Michael Dean Perry, who starred at Aiken S.C. High School before going on to fame at Clemson University and the National Football League. Hixon recalls that on several occasions, the Fridge, then in elementary and middle school, traveled with the Eagles team bus on road games.

Atlanta area semi-pro players

Steve Wilder, *J.J., Mean Machine;* **George A. Jones,** *Big George, Mean Machine;* **Wilbur Gilliam,** *Big Wilbur, Mean Machine.*

“...a director’s chair next to Burt’s...”

Gator

Donnie kept in touch with Burt Reynolds after *The Longest Yard,* and three years later visited him in Savannah for the filming of *Gator,* another prison-themed movie and Reynolds' first attempt as a film director. Augusta Eagles owner Dr. Gus Carlucci and two others had driven to the film set and tried in vain to get inside the ropes. The next day, Carlucci invited Hixon to join them as their "sure ticket" to visit with Burt. Donnie joined Dr. Carlucci, Eagles coach Tom Goforth, and local standout Wade Brantley on the excursion and arrived in Savannah shortly after lunch, when filming had resumed for the afternoon.

Reynolds' hair stylist and makeup man recognized Hixon from their *Longest Yard* days, and told the group of Augustans he'd be right back. Several minutes later, Reynolds appeared, and amidst the masses screaming for his attention, signaled Hixon only inside the ropes. According to Hixon, Burt met him with that "I'm glad to see you smile of his, a handshake, and grabbed me around my shoulders as we walked back inside where he was directing..." Hixon was accorded a director's chair next to Burt's, where he watched Reynolds direct a fight scene inside a bar for the movie.

Also on hand were Longest Yard actors Don Ferguson, Wilbur J.J. Wilder, Sonny Shroyer, and John "Pop" Steadman who also had parts in Gator. In between breaks, the Augusta group hung out with actor and singer Jerry Reed, who Hixon remembers as "full of life, very funny, and entertaining to be around, just like you would expect!" Donnie also had his picture taken with NFL great Alex Hawkins, who played the role of the police chief in the movie. Hawkins was captain of the Baltimore Colts special teams in Super Bowl III, when Joe Namath's New York Jets bested the Colts 16-7.

Among the crowd of actors and extras in Savannah were Jack Weston and actress Lauren Hutton. The following day, Burt cast Hixon as an extra in a scene in Gator and told Donnie he might be able to find a small part for him in the film. Gracious for the opportunity, Hixon kindly refused the offer and informed Reynolds that he couldn't get the time off. In the three years since the filming of *The Longest Yard,* Hixon had been promoted to head up his company's offices in a three-state area that included South Carolina. And since he'd already been the stunt double for the top actor on planet Earth, Hixon had long since marked movie star off his lifetime bucket list. "When the wrap was over that day," says Donnie, "I stopped by Burt's Winnebago... thanked him, and said good-bye!" The following day, at Donnie's office in Augusta, Hixon took a phone call from an ecstatic Dr. Carlucci, who let him know that Burt had cast him in *Gator* as a doctor, to play the role of none other than "Dr. Carlucci."

An Evening with Burt Reynolds

Nearly 40 years had passed since Burt Reynolds and Donnie Hixon donned identical #22 jerseys for filming of *The Longest Yard* at Reidsville State Prison. In late March 2013, Burt was scheduled to appear for two nights at the famed Lyric Theatre in downtown Stuart, Florida. Despite having undergone total knee replacement surgery on his left leg just two weeks prior, Hixon was determined to make the 500-mile trip from Augusta. "The trip was the most miserable one I'd been on," says Hixon, who traveled with wife Beverly, who had heard the stories but had yet to meet Reynolds. Donnie forwarded a note to Burt a week before the show to let him know he'd be in the audience that night.

First, Hixon would need to endure an agonizing ride on construction-ridden, wreck-prone Interstate 95. In order to prevent a blood clot, he was instructed by his orthopedic surgeon to keep the leg iced, and to stop and stretch at one-hour intervals. Countless traffic delays turned the scheduled seven and a half hour journey on a good day into a 12-hour odyssey this day. When the Hixons finally arrived at the home of friends Lois and Al Hutko in Plant City, Donnie was near tears, torn between the pain in his leg and joy in his heart for surviving the trip. "The next morning my knee was all swollen, and I was in some pain," recalls Hixon. As he would soon find out, his old friend Burt was hurting even more than he was.

At the Lyric Theatre that night, ushers made sure to seat the Hixons so Burt could see them, and Burt sent word that he was aware of their arrival and would contact them following the performance. But it was obvious to the 500 in attendance that night, that when Reynolds entered the theatre stage, he was in pain. "He came out, moving slowly, and having to walk with the use of a cane," said Hixon, who also limped into the Lyric that night with the use of a cane. Once seated, Reynolds addressed both the audience and a large movie screen at center stage. After clips of the movies he starred in were shown onscreen, Reynolds told stories about the characters and backstories of each. Burt utilized his cane as a prop to signal the next film clip to be seen onscreen.

Then Hixon watched as Reynolds struggled to return to the backstage dressing room for intermission, during which he was informed that Burt was not feeling well and might not be able to continue with the remainder of the scheduled performance. But this was Burt Reynolds, the one-time box-office sensation, the star athlete who played in pain. He would not let pain get in the way of performance. After the break, and a full theatre had returned to their seats, Reynolds slowly reappeared.

The Lyric Theatre had strict rules, much like the Masters Tournament in Augusta, and no pictures could be taken during the performance. The Lyric also prohibited patrons from leaving their seats and approaching the stage, but Hixon broke the rules that night and headed up to the stage. "When I got up there, he saw me and came over to see me," relates Hixon. "Face to face with him, shaking hands with him," Hixon says he told the aging star, "I love you Burt, you are my hero." and that Burt responded in kind, "I love you Donnie and you are my hero!" Standing there, close up, with their canes and grey hair, the audience could see the resemblance, as they had in the famous film in which each wore #22, four decades earlier. Those in attendance politely waited on the slight interruption and whispered that Hixon must be Reynolds' brother.

As the audience looked on, Reynolds told Hixon that he suffered from constant pain everyday, from nine major operations and 30 broken bones (the result of stunts during his acting career.) It was obvious to Hixon that Father Time and countless pain medications had taken a toll on Reynolds. "I almost cried looking at him that way, remembering what a handsome, muscular person he was during the filming of *The Longest Yard*... In his day, he would probably run through a brick wall. But now..." Hixon surmised, "He looked like he wasn't going to be around much longer." All the while, Hixon's wife, Beverly, elbowed her husband, and beckoned, *"Introduce me! Introduce me!"* After a proper introduction, the Hixons headed back to their seats, and Burt returned to the stage.

Like the football star he was at West Palm Beach High and again at Florida State, where a knee injury cut short his athletic career, Reynolds learned early in life to play through the pain, and even hide it, if need be. Maybe he could even find a way to mask the pain during the packed performance at the Lyric Theatre that night, the cheers and smiling faces serving to numb what medication no longer could. It was after the clapping stopped that the pain flooded back, seemingly double the amount he was able to hold back at center stage.

At the end of the performance, the Hixons were instructed to remain seated until the audience cleared. Then they were reseated, along with their friends, the Hutkos, on the front row nearest the stage door, and informed that Burt would be out shortly to greet them all. The group was ecstatic for the chance to meet with Reynolds. But backstage, Reynolds was not feeling well and the group was updated that he was being attended to. It would be a bit longer before he would be out to see them, they were told. A short while later, a member of Burt's production crew informed the group that Reynolds had taken ill and was too sick to see them. "I still remember hearing her say that and it hit me like air going out of a hot air balloon," Hixon said. Though they were naturally disappointed, they were equally sorry to hear Burt was not feeling well. Number 22 had given his all. A couple of weeks later, Burt had the manager send Hixon a copy of his book, My Life, that he had autographed.

Return to Reidsville

On the crisp, sunny morning of February 1, 2018, Donnie Hixon returned to Reidsville Prison for the first time in nearly half a century and I accompanied him to document the visit. Memories flooded Hixon's mind as he recounted his first day at the prison, in 1973. It was Hixon's Paramount Pictures ID card, and a scrapbook full of rare photos from the production that played a large part in getting us inside the prison. One look at Hixon's old ID and Warden Marty Allen knew this was something he hadn't encountered before. Sure, he had seen the pictures on the fifth floor prison walls that documented the event, but never had anyone shown up looking to get inside the prison to relive those days. The warden quipped that Hixon's 45-year-old ID card came without an expiration date, then made a few phone calls and warmly welcomed Burt Reynolds' stunt double back to Reidsville for a tour.

High atop the prison, one floor up from death row, rests a small room that houses the now obsolete electric chair, one that was still in use when *The Longest Yard* was filmed. A barred window not far from the chair overlooks the one-time field put in place for the production. The movie's original script and countless pictures from those days are located along the walls in that same room. The small room represents a bygone era — where in stark contrast, both the happiest and saddest moments in the prison's 82-year history share space not more than 20 feet apart. Then it's back through the narrow, winding staircase and cramped walkways at the top of the prison to much wider staircases that tumble down to the first floor. There, Warden Allen proudly showed off his Georgia Bulldogs office chair before escorting Hixon and I back outside the facility.

During the ride back home to Augusta, Donnie shared these comments with this author: "Amazing, (that's) all I've got to say. That was real interesting, especially looking at that electric chair where so many people died. And then looking at that phone on the wall where in case the governor calls — you've got to imagine what was going through their mind..."

The stories Hixon tells of Reidsville speak to a time when he and the cast he worked alongside were young, and could take a hit and bounce back to their feet. For Donnie Hixon and Burt Reynolds and Ray Nitschke and the cast and crew of *The Longest Yard,* the fall of 1973 at Reidsville Prison was life changing — *the time of their lives!*

As we drove through the town of Reidville, the sun through the window lit up Hixon's face and from time to time cast a silhouette. I remarked to Donnie at the time, "I can see a little Burt in you right now. If the light is just right and we head back 45 years, nearly half a century, I definitely can see a little Burt there." Hixon replied, "I wish I looked like that. (long pause) Time takes care of everybody. It got me."

Joe Jackson Funeral

Just two months after Donnie's return to Reidsville, Joe Jackson, the running back who took *The Longest Yard* by storm, passed away in Atlanta on Easter Sunday, April 1, 2018. Jackson was buried in his hometown of Augusta just over two weeks later. His old coach and friend from the Augusta Eagles, Donnie Hixon, was asked to speak at Jackson's funeral. Hixon also worked behind the scenes to raise funeral expense money in the Laney community where Jackson once starred in high school in an effort to make sure his friend and teammate in *The Longest Yard* went out in style. Hixon even provided a new light blue sport coat, white shirt, tie, underwear and socks for Jackson's funeral service. Some men will give you the shirt off their back. In a symbolic gesture to both Jackson and Burt Reynolds, who respected Joe Jack's immense talent, Hixon did one better. He dressed Jackson in a pair of his own navy slacks that he had worn just once – the time he visited Burt Reynolds for the last time in Stuart, Florida in 2013.

Hixon also appealed to Minister Carl L. Jones that Jackson's funeral service be altered to allow for him to speak last at the ceremony. Minister Jones obliged Hixon. Known for his motivation of both football players and employees, and no stranger to most of those in attendance, he didn't speak from his pew as others did prior to him, rather, Hixon strode to the podium as the final speaker. "Let me tell you something," said Hixon's longtime friend, Don Tyre, who was also in attendance, "Donnie took command of the situation." Hixon was upbeat as he talked about his former teammate on the Mean Machine and player he coached with the Augusta Eagles. Hixon shared stories about how well Joe Jack performed against former NFL stars during production of *The Longest Yard* some 45 years earlier.

According to Tyre, "Donnie started, and got his second wind and he'd say things that were funny and he'd get them laughing, and that really fired up Donnie that much more. He had the whole congregation in the palm of his hand when he got through." During one such story, the entire assembly at Gibson Chapel in the C.A. Reid., Sr. Memorial Funeral Home in Augusta fell silent when Hixon disagreed with other speakers at the ceremony that Joe was well liked by all. Hixon had the stunned congregation's undivided attention. Then he proceeded to relate that Jackson was not liked by players on opposing semipro football teams who had previously been punished by the the powerful running back.

Most, if not all those in attendance, knew of Jackson's legend while playing football at nearby Laney High School, where he gained a scholarship to Maryland State. Courtesy of Donnie Hixon, Jackson's 15 minutes of fame came in *The Longest Yard.* When you watch the movie, pay close attention to #29, the running back that Hixon recruited and Burt Reynolds was so impressed with that he tagged him with the nickname "Joe Jack." Jackson never forgot the gesture.

Jackson's first cousin Gloria Jean Shanks, whom he lived with for several years in Santa Ana, California, said "He (Joe) was crazy about Donnie. He said Donnie introduced him to Burt (Reynolds) and he got to be part of his movie. They would talk about Burt and the movie they made, and how he got into the movie." She also confided that "He (Donnie) put up with Joe a lot... Joe called Donnie because he knew Donnie would listen to him no matter what... Many people wouldn't have taken that time with Joe... he knew Donnie was there for him."

Hixon announced to those in attendance at Jackson's funeral that that they were not going to end the service on a somber note, that his good friend, Jackson, would not have wanted it that way. Hixon urged the attendees to their feet and to give it up for the truly well-liked Joe Jackson. With that the group was on its feet chanting and whooping it up, for they knew in their hearts that Joe Jack was one of the greatest athletes ever to play sports in the community, maybe any community. Five months after "Joe Jack's" passing, the man who gave Jackson his nickname, Burt Reynolds died on September 6, 2018. "A Celebration of the Life of Burt Reynolds," a private service honoring the famous actor, was held in West Palm Beach, Florida on Wednesday, September 20, 2018.

“...Donnie
was a
legend...”

Accolades

The Longest Yard changed Hixon's life in three areas – it boosted his self esteem after years of struggle in his youth, it provided lessons learned that he could utilize when coaching the Augusta Eagles, and it aided in his managerial skills aimed at motivating his employees to become the best they could be.

"A shining light from the darkness of stress and hardships that most people never experience. Donnie was a legend and a measuring stick we all wanted to live up to..." is the way friend and musician Sammy O'Banion, Richmond Academy Class of 1968, and Carolina Beach Music Association Hall of Fame summed up Hixon.

Longtime friend, Don Tyre says of Hixon – *"He was a good Marine and athlete. He's a standup, class guy. If you need him, he'll be there for you."*

Sharon Moore, who worked with Donnie as a Senior VP with Fleet Finance and Mortgage relates that Donnie is an *"outstanding leader and motivator! Great speaker and personality, second to nobody – very professional... He would stand up for what was right, at a time when it was not popular to do so."*

In an unsolicited voicemail Hixon retrieved from his telephone on November 22, 2018, from Steve Reed, a mortgage broken who Donnie mentored, *"Man, when I think about being grateful for something, with Thanksgiving coming up tomorrow... wow – I think about you and what you poured into me as a young person... and all your life lessons, and all your wisdom."*

Excerpted a letter sent to Hixon by Victor Ramierez, a student he mentored at Lakeside High School in Columbia County, Georgia, in 2013, *"First of all, I want to say that you're an amazing man. You've changed my view of life in so many ways... Our talks have kept me out of a lot of trouble. You have motivated me not to take life for granted and to keep my attitude positive... The environment you grew up in and the way you handle it gives me no reason to slack off. You have inspired me to have a work ethic unlike others and to help people who are in need..."*

In an article that appeared in *The Augusta Chronicle-Herald,* July 12, 1987, former Augusta Eagle head coach Harvey Hogan, whom Hixon played for in 1968 and 1969 was quoted as having said: *"Donnie was a winner. He could move the ball. It was like having a coach on the field. He could find ways to win."*

No one likely summed it up better than Georgia football great and Auburn coaching legend, Pat Dye, when he signed a photograph to Hixon, *"Donnie, You Beat All The Odds."*

The Longest Yard Synopsis

*To say the finished product was a smash hit with moviegoers would be putting it mildly. Hollywood cashed in big as the low-budget production grossed 43 million dollars in receipts. With similar box-office numbers in back-to-back movies, (*Deliverance, *1972, and* The Longest Yard, *1974), (Burt) Reynolds cemented his name as a bona-fide leading man. Hixon's life also changed dramatically as his persona was suddenly, and forevermore connected to Reynolds. "I never met anybody like that before, with that notoriety... It kind of changed my life, I took on a new identity," says Hixon. 'Today I went to Walmart, a guy came up to me and introduced me to his wife and said, 'He's the one who did* The Longest Yard.' *I get it all the time, it never stops."*

1974's *The Longest Yard,* though irreverent and not politically correct, is regarded by many as the best sports movie of all time. The movie's producer, Albert S. Ruddy, came up with the storyline and Tracy Keenan Wynn penned the screenplay. Alan Horowitz served as the film's associate producer.

The star-studded production, with former NFL players and rising Hollywood stars, was filmed in the autumn of 1973 at Reidsville State

Prison, a maximum security facility in south Georgia. For the purposes of the film, the location was renamed Citrus State Prison in Florida. The movie centers on Paul "Wrecking" Crewe (Burt Reynolds), a disgraced former NFL player, who is sentenced to 18 months at the lockdown for taking his well-to-do girlfriend's Maserati for a joyride and dumping it into the Atlantic ocean in a fit of rage.

Kicked out of the league for point shaving, Crewe's checkered past is a fact not lost on ruthless Citrus State Warden Rudolph Hazen (Eddie Albert). On the side, the football-crazed warden also finds time to manage a semi-pro football team comprised of prison guards. The warden seeks out Crewe, first to enlist him as a coach, which Reynolds' character declines, then to form a ragtag group of inmates to serve as whipping boys for his Guards' team. Crewe declines further, but persuasive Guards' Captain Wilhelm Knauer (Ed Lauter) eventually gets Crewe to rethink his original stance and take part in an exhibition game, guards versus the inmates.

With the aid of Caretaker (James Hampton), Crewe enlists his first two players, former pro weightlifter Samson (Richard Kiel), and Connie Shockner (Robert Tessier), a serial killer turned martial arts expert. When coach Nate Scarboro (Michael Conrad), and Granny Granville (Harry Caesar), the first black inmate on the team, who like Crewe is a former professional player, and Pop (John Steadman) join, the inmates' team begins to take shape.

The other #22 in the movie, Burt Reynolds' stunt double Donnie Hixon, relates that "The selling point to the convicts was that it was their chance to punish and get back at those harassing guards. That was music to their ears as they couldn't wait to get on the field and inflict pain on the guards. This was now building up to be a knock down drag out violent game between the prison guards and convicts!"

Crewe's decision to quarterback the team gives the inmates a fighting chance. After Granny is hassled by prison guards, additional black inmates cast their lots with Crewe, and the team quickly evolves into a force to be reckoned with.

In a critical scene in the movie, Crewe reveals his intentions for playing against the Guards to Nate Scarboro, coach of the Mean Machine. "Nate, if you're thinking about winning this game, then you're as crazy as he (Hazen) is." To which Scarboro replies, "Well, maybe so. But you spend fourteen years in this tank, you begin to understand that you've only got two things left they can't sweat out of you or beat out of you... Your balls. And you better hang onto them because they're about the only thing you're gonna have when you get out of here."

When Crewe rejects overtures by prison insider and conniving weasel Unger (Charles Tyner) to take Caretaker's position as team manager, the scorned inmate retaliates. Unger's attempt to kill off Burt Reynolds' character with a self-concocted lightbulb bomb fatally injures Caretaker instead. The death of the beloved Caretaker only serves to unify the inmates, and the film's intensity ratchets up significantly when the Mean Machine emerges on game day sporting uniforms stolen from the Guards by Caretaker prior to his death. Game on!

The inspired Mean Machine plays the first half within two points (15-13) of the Guards, too close for comfort for the heartless warden Hazen, who appeals to Crewe's checkered past and delivers an ultimatum to Burt Reynolds' character. Crewe must orchestrate a 21-point Mean Machine loss to the Guards or be fingered as an accessory in Caretakers murder, with Unger as witness. Faced with such a life-altering decision, Crewe reluctantly agrees to the scheme, but only on the condition that Hazen's Guards cause no physical harm to the prison team during the second half of the contest. The fix is in.

Reduced to a puppet, and his team no better than pawns, Crewe turns suddenly inept at quarterback as the Guards march to the prearranged point spread. Once the lead is secured, the callous Warden Hazen goes back on his word and instructs Captain Knauer to "inflict as much physical punishment on the prisoners as humanly possible." The proud and unwitting Mean Machine fights on until it becomes obvious of Crewe's real intentions to help fix the game. But incensed by Knauer's move to hurt his players, Crewe has a change of heart and Crewe returns to the lineup late in the game. Crewe manages to win back the confidence of the Mean Machine, which regroups to pull within five points of the Guards, 35-30.

In the waning moments, and down to their last chance, the Mean Machine's Scarboro sustains a crippling injury courtesy of Guard Bogdanski (Ray Nitschke, Green Bay Packers fame). Scarboro makes one final plea to Crewe as he is carted off the field, "Paul, you've got to do it. Screw Hazen." In reply, Crewe says, "Don't worry, he'll get his." Inspired by his team's refusal to give up, Crewe rallies his team late in the game. With the Guards leading 35-30, and the Mean Machine with the ball at the one yard line and facing 4th and one with seven seconds remaining, Crewe calls time and huddles up with the entire team. One one knee, and his jersey in shreds, he looks up into the huddle and says, "We've come too far together to stop now. For Granny, for Mick, (pause), for Caretaker. Let's do it!"

According to Hixon, the final play of the game was shot numerous times. For dramatic effect, the play is run in slow motion, as Crewe spins and sweeps to the right before changing directions in a play that runs one minute, 22 seconds onscreen. Crewe finally hurdles into the end zone just after time expires to give the Mean Machine a 36-35 victory! As Crewe walks across the field to pick up the game ball during the ensuing celebration, Hazen repeatedly orders Knauer to shoot him on the grounds that Crewe is trying to escape. But Knauer, won over by Crewe's display of gamesmanship, holds off in carrying out the warden's orders. Crewe picks up the football, and walks it back to Hazen as Knauer remarks "Game ball" and turns to walk away. Enter Crewe, who walks up smiling, deposits the ball firmly in the warden's hands, and remarks, "Stick this in your trophy case!"

The actual recipe that went into making the iconic motion picture at Reidsville had gone something like this: Carefully select a dozen or so choice Hollywood stars, add a dozen seasoned former NFL standouts and make room for fifteen of Hixon's teammates from the Augusta Eagles football team. Get Governor Jimmy Carter's stamp of approval to utilize the maximum security prison at Reidsville. Stir slowly and sprinkle with inmates (who auditioned for and won roles in the film), and top things off with a Hollywood production crew. Place in the pressure cooker at Reidsville and bake for nine weeks at South Georgia temperatures. Contain the mixture within a perimeter of razor sharp wire – and be sure not to let boil over!!! Remove and serve hot to moviegoers worldwide, popcorn optional.

“...Never in my dreams did I think I would be playing...”

The Longest Yard Character Bios

Robert Aldrich, *Director*

Born into privilege, Aldrich dropped out of the University of Virginia in 1941 to work in a menial capacity at RKO Pictures. His family threatened to cut him off from a potential inheritance stake in Chase Bank, but Aldrich never looked back, and carved out a successful career as a Hollywood director and producer. A letterman on the 1940 UVA football team, Aldrich, like Burt Reynolds, suffered injuries to his knees and both were given opportunities to reconnect with the sport of their youth in the making of *The Longest Yard*. In short order, Aldrich and Reynolds teamed up for another box office sensation with *Hustle* (1975). Among Aldrich's many directing credits are *Vera Cruz* (1954), *Whatever Happened to Baby Jane?* (1962), *Hush... Hush, Sweet Charlotte* (1964), and *The Dirty Dozen* (1967). Aldrich died in 1983.

#22 Donnie Hixon remembers *"Mr. Aldrich was the one running the show for* The Longest Yard. *He was very nice, in his fifties at the time, and looked like he enjoyed eating good meals – he was solid, but a little on the heavy side. It was an honor and very exciting to have been around such a great man, and watching him direct the movie. Plus knowing he was the* *film director of the movie,* The Dirty Dozen *featuring pro-football great Jim Brown and other great actors. He did pay compliments to me a few times saying, 'Donnie, you make a great double!' Coming from someone with his resume, that was a great compliment. Ten years after the filming of* The Longest Yard, *I sadly heard on the news that Mr. Aldrich had passed away at age 65. Any time news came on the TV or radio that was associated with the movie, I always paid special attention. Mr. Aldrich looked like and acted like a football coach, was always on top of what was going on, and in charge. Listening to him and watching his demeanor and personality while he was directing made me believe he was a super nice person, family man, and a great role model. He was a special person to work for!"*

Albert S. Ruddy, *Producer*

Ruddy got his break in the film industry when Marlon Brando's dad hired him to produce *Wild Seed* (1965). With momentum in his favor, he followed up with the television hit, *Hogan's Heroes* (1965-1971), which he co-originated for CBS. Ruddy won the first of two Academy Awards for Best Picture with the blockbuster hit, *The Godfather* (1972), in which Burt Reynolds turned down the part of Michael Corleone. In short order, Ruddy produced the box office sensation, *The Longest Yard* (1974), which sports writer Bill Simmons cited as "the best football movie of all-time. Hands down," and "the first successful modern sports movie." The production proved so popular that it was remade twice, both with Ruddy as producer, as the *Mean Machine* (2001), and again in 2005 under its original name with Adam Sandler in the lead and Burt Reynolds as Coach Nate Scarborough. Ruddy added two more hits with Reynolds, *Cannonball Run* (1981) and the followup, *Cannonball Run II* (1984), and went on to claim a second Oscar® for Best Picture with his production of *Million Dollar Baby* (2004).

Eddie Albert, *Warden Hazen*

Albert's role as Warden Hazen in *The Longest Yard* came on the heels of his second Oscar® nomination for Best Supporting Actor, from his role as Mr. Corcoran in the 1972 release of *The Heartbreak Kid.* His performance as Irving Radovich in a supporting role in 1953's *Roman Holiday* also earned an Academy nomination. Albert, who died at the age of 99 in 2005, starred in the early days of television, in the early to mid-1960s, as Oliver Wendell Douglas in *Green Acres.*

#22 Donnie Hixon remembers *"Some days after eating lunch in the picnic area outside the prison, he came back inside the prison right away to walk around the football field. This gave me the opportunity on several occasions to have one-on-one conversations while walking with him. He didn't volunteer much information about himself but what I did pull out of him was very interesting. I remember him saying he liked to play the guitar. He seemed like a very serious person.*

Pervis Atkins, *Mawabe (Mean Machine)*

At New Mexico State, in 1959, Atkins led the nation in rushing with 971 yards. The following year, when teammate Bob Gaiters won the rushing title, Atkins led the nation with 9.4 yards per carry. Then it was off to the National Football League for six seasons with three teams, the Rams (1961-1963), the Redskins (1964-1965), and Raiders (1965-1966). Atkins was named to the College Football Hall of Fame in 2009 and died in Los Angeles at the age 82 in December, 2017.

#22 Donnie Hixon remembers *"Pervis was a super nice, very friendly and intelligent person who had a great smile that said 'I'm glad to see you,' no matter who you were. He had a great personality. I always enjoyed talking with him about his football journey, and football stories in general. He wore jersey #17 and was a flanker for the Mean Machine. He was a great athlete who could turn it up a notch when it* *came to speed. Never in my dreams did I ever think I would be playing and throwing a football to someone who had a resume like his. He still had great moves and hands catching the football. Pervis looked like, and ran like, a track star."*

Tony Cacciotti, *Rotka (Mean Machine)*

Cacciotti earned credits in two movies, as Rotka in *The Longest Yard,* and Anthony Casselli in *Hero at Large* (1980). He also appeared in an episode of the *Dukes of Hazzard* television show in 1979. Cacciotti scored a credit as a producer for the movie, *Golda's Balcony,* in which his wife in real life, Valerie Harper stars.

Harry Caesar, *Granville (Mean Machine)*

Born in Pittsburgh in 1928, Harry Caesar was a latecomer to the film industry. He was 41 years of age when he made his debut. From then on, he proved a mainstay in film and television for nearly a quarter century beginning in 1969. Five years later, his role as Granville in *The Longest Yard* showed a small spotlight on Caesar, who went on to accumulate 59 film and television credits in his career. His memorable lines in *The Longest Yard* were a well-timed declaration to his teammates on the Mean Machine, "Alright men, now here's the play we're gonna use. I don't think the guards know this formation. It's called 'incidental punishment after the ball is blown dead.' Remember, any man you tackle gets an elbow, knee, or kick in the mouth." Caesar also earned accolades for his roles as Marvin in *Bird on a Wire* (1990) and Luther in *A Few Good Men* (1992). Caesar died at the age of 66 in Los Angeles County in 1994.

#22 Donnie Hixon remembers *"Harry had acting roles in the movie, but was not involved in action in the live football scrimmages that I remember. He was a very pleasant and gentle person who had a good attitude. He always had a big smile on his face, the type of person who* *looked like they wouldn't harm or hurt anyone. He had some great speaking parts in the movie."*

Cheerleaders

#22 Donnie Hixon remembers *"The cheerleaders who performed in the movie were prisoners who supposedly were gay. The Paramount wardrobe personnel dressed them up in their outfits big time. Half of them were in silk tight-fitting maroon shorts and yellow tops, and the others wore black and silver outfits. Whenever we broke for lunch they would practice during that hour. Most of the time we came back inside with time left on the lunch clock and listened to them practice, or we played Joe Kapp's grab-ass football, or his instant replay rehearsal, or just sat around on the field. They danced to the music of 'Shot Gun' Morgan, who was the leader of the prison band in the movie. Man could they dance. They were very talented and entertaining.*

"When halftime came in the film, actor Michael Fox, the game announcer, called their show in the movie, 'The Gala Halftime Activities.' The wardrobe department had Shot Gun looking like a real band leader in those clothes. He wore a tailor-made ivory-colored coat that buttoned down the middle, with gold buttons in front, which were also on each sleeve. He also wore a coat similar to a Nehru-style hip length jacket with a mandarin (short unfolded stand-up) collar. There was only one epaulet on the right shoulder of the jacket that had a French fourragere decorative braided knotted cord that looped through the epaulet and under the arm. This is usually worn on the left shoulder and awarded to military units. He also wore black trousers with a gold stripe down the outside of each leg.

"The cheerleaders and dancers were not allowed down on the field with us, only Shot Gun was privileged to be down on the field. After having been around him a few times I asked him 'What kind of trouble did you get into that put you in this jail?' He said he was in for premeditated murder.

I said, 'You've got to be kidding, you don't seem like the type, and you must have had a good reason.' He said he got bullied, attacked, and beat up badly by three others. Afterwards he went home, got the family shot gun, returned, shot them, killing two of them. Now you know why the prison inmates nicknamed him Shot Gun Morgan! He made a bad choice and was paying the price for it!

"The life-learning lesson from this is to stop and think – don't let rage and anger cause you to take the law into your own hands. I told him I made a stupid choice once when I stole some hubcaps I thought were mine. I told him I got arrested later on in the day, spent three nights in jail, and my sentence was four years – the judge made me join the Marines. I was very lucky I didn't get shot. I should have called the police if I thought they were mine, and let them investigate the matter."

Michael Conrad, *Nate Scarboro (Mean Machine)*

The talented Conrad played character roles in scores of television and film productions. He is likely best known for his acting in the highly acclaimed television series, *Hill Street Blues*, in which played the role of Phil Esterhaus. Conrad won two Emmys (1981,1982) for Outstanding Supporting Actor in a Drama Series for his work on the primetime show. Conrad played an equally memorable role in *The Longest Yard* as Nate Scarboro, coach of the Mean Machine.

#22 Donnie Hixon remembers *"I remember him looking like a highly sophisticated, tall and handsome man who was very friendly and easy to talk with. He was first class, very professional. Another one who always had that look on his face, 'It's so good to see you.' He did no coaching, only played the part of the coach in the movie. Joe Kapp was the one who coached and organized us in football. I used* *to walk up to (Conrad) kidding around sometime saying, 'Send me in, coach, give me the ball!' He would just laugh with a great big smile on his face!"*

Anitra Ford, *Melissa*

Best known for her role as a television model alongside game show host Bob Barker on *The Price Is Right,* Ford played Burt Reynolds' girlfriend in *The Longest Yard.*

Michael Fox, *Annnouncer*

(Not to be confused with Michael J. Fox) The indefatigable Fox appeared in over 200 television and film productions in a career that spanned more than four decades. Included in his myriad of credits is that of the football game announcer in *The Longest Yard.* Fox passed away at the age of 75 at Woodland Hills, California in 1996.

James Hampton, *Caretaker (Mean Machine)*

With numerous television and film credits, Hampton made his film debut in *The Cliff Dwellers* (1962) and the production was nominated for an Academy Award® in the short subject category. In his very next role he starred with Burt Reynolds in the first of three appearances he would make in the *Gunsmoke* television series. In 1976, Hampton received a HALO Award for the western comedy, *Hawmps!*

Hampton's memorable role as Caretaker in *The Longest Yard* earned him a Golden Globe nomination for Most Promising Newcomer. His performance included an exchange with Paul Crewe (Burt Reynolds), the quarterback of the Mean Machine and whose character had been kicked out of the NFL for point-shaving, "Most of these old boys don't have nothing. Never had nothing to start with. But you, you had it all. Then you let your teammates down, got yourself caught with your hand in the cookie jar... Oh I ain't saying you did or you didn't. All I'm saying is that you could have robbed banks, sold dope or stole your grandmother's pension checks and none of us would have minded. But shaving points off of a football game, man that's un-American."

Mike Henry, *Rassmeusen (Guards)*

Born in Los Angeles, Henry was a standout linebacker at the University of Southern California in college prior to an NFL career that spanned six seasons, (1958-1964). In the National Football League, he played three years each with the Pittsburgh Steelers and hometown Los Angeles Rams, and was under contract with Warner Brothers during the latter half of his career. In an acting career that includes two dozen films, Henry is best known for his role in three Tarzan movies, *Tarzan and the Valley of Gold* (1966), *Tarzan and the Great River* (1967), and *Tarzan and the Jungle Boy* (1968). He appeared in two dozen films during his acting career, and after his role as a prison guard in *The Longest Yard*, was cast in all three *Smokey and the Bandit* movies (1977, 1980, 1983) that starred Burt Reynolds and Sally Field.

#22 Donnie Hixon remembers *"...Mike seemed like a very happy person, easygoing, great to talk with, and a joy to be around. I remember him as being very tall, dark haired, and very muscular. Someone told me he played Tarzan in the movies. In conversation with him, I asked if it was true. He said it was true, that he played in three Tarzan films in the 60's... We got to talking about his college football days at USC and when he played linebacker for the Pittsburgh Steelers and Los Angeles Rams. He said he was discovered by Warner Brothers while playing for the Rams, and that's how his acting career got started. Not many people make the claim that they got to meet and hang out with Tarzan, but I can. Mike Henry was Tarzan!"*

Joe Kapp, *Walking Boss (Guards)*

A member of the Canadian and College Football Halls of Fame, Joe

Kapp had the rare opportunity to quarterback in a Super Bowl, Grey Cup, and Rose Bowl. And his #22 jersey (the same number worn by Reynolds in *The Longest Yard*) was retired by the British Columbia Lions, the team he led to the Grey Cup in 1964. In 1969, Kapp led the Minnesota Vikings to the last NFL Championship ever played, though the Vikings lost to Kansas City in Super Bowl IV. During his college career, Kapp quarterbacked the University of California, Berkeley, to the Pacific Coast Championship in 1958, and a berth in the 1959 New Year's Day Rose Bowl. He returned to his alma mater as head coach between 1982-1986.

#22 Donnie Hixon remembers *"Joe was a tall, good-looking guy known for his reputation of playing no matter how beat up he was, he still played with toughness and remained a fierce competitor.... it is obvious you couldn't help but notice the fight in him, competitiveness, and no fear at all cost, and the will to win! He was full of piss and vinegar! You could see he played to win, always giving it his all."*

Richard "Dick" Kiel, *Samson (Mean Machine)*

Born in Detroit in 1939 with a hormonal condition known as acromegaly, the 7'4" Kiel's acting career also spanned great heights. A mainstay of film and television for half a century, Kiel played Samson in *The Longest Yard*. His memorable scene in the movie is when he stiff-arms a Guards running back and remarks "I think I broke his f****** neck!" He is best known for his role as Jaws in a pair of James Bond films, *The Spy Who Loved Me* (1977) and *Moonraker* (1979). Kiel's credits include appearances in 34 films and 50 television episodes. Kiel passed away in 2014, just shy of his 75th birthday.

#22 Donnie Hixon remembers *"There is a scene in* The Longest Yard *in which Burt Reynolds recruits Kiel's character, Samson, to play* *against the Guards team. Samson, who is lifting weights with 300 pounds on each end, growls 'I would like that,' and reaches down with both hands, grabs the bar, and lets out a deep growl as he jerks and lifts the bar and weights above his shoulders Hollywood style: fake weights!*

"About three weeks or so later, Neil Leifer, a well-known sports photographer, paid a visit to Reidville, along with Emily McLendon, who wrote a story covering the movie in the year-ending Sports Illustrated issue of December 30, 1974. This presented an opportunity to play a trick on Kiel by some of the movie crew members, who took the fake weights, and replaced them with real ones. Kiel was informed that Sports Illustrated *wanted a picture of him lifting the weights for the magazine. He was all excited, and when there was a break in the regular filming, they motioned for him to get in position, and be ready to be photographed.*

"When they hollered 'action,' the big guy bent down in the squat position, grabbed hold of the bar with both hands, and let out a growl before attempting. After failing to lift up the bar with the real weights the first time, he tried a second and his hands slipped off the bar and caused him to fall backwards where he landed on his butt in the sitting position! While we were all standing there laughing, you should have seen the look on his face. The big smile and look on his face let us know that he knew he'd been had, and he started laughing along with us. Being a good-natured person, he was a good sport about it."

Ed Lauter, Captain Knauer (Guards)

The versatile Lauter is credited with character appearances in 220 film and television productions over a storied 40-year career. A basketball player in college, Lauter's acting and athleticism came to light in *The Longest Yard,* in his role as the maniacal prison guard team's Captain Knauer. In the film's climactic scene, Knauer holds a rifle as Warden Hazen barks orders at him to shoot Crewe. The memorable performance served as a launching pad in Lauter's career. In 2005, Lauter appeared with Reynolds in the movie's remake, with Adam Sandler in the lead role. Lauter died in October, 2017 — some forty years after the original *The Longest Yard* was filmed.

#22 Donnie Hixon remembers *"Watching him act reminded me of my Marine Drill Instructors at Parris Island! He would have made a great one, he was that good! He could portray such a mean person, yet was so nice when not acting. It was like he had two personalities. What an actor! Through the years I've enjoyed watching him play that badass mean person in several movies. If provoked, in my opinion, I bet he would be a scrapper in a street fight. He gave me the impression if a fight broke out, he was the type of friend you could count on to have your back!"*

Mort Marshall, *Assistant Warden*

Though his film credits include only a dozen titles, Marshall appeared in two other Robert Aldrich films, *Kiss Me Deadly* (1955), and *The Grisom Gang* (1971), and three additional movies with Burt Reynolds, *Skullduggery* (1970), *W.W. and the Dixie Dancekings* (1975), and *Starting Over* (1979). Marshall also had a successful career as a voice actor in three animated children's TV shows, including the voice of Klondike Kat (1966). In television commercials, he was the original voice of the Trix Rabbit. Marshall died in 1979 at the age of 60.

Pepper Martin, *Shop Steward (Mean Machine)*

The Canadian-born Martin first made a name for himself in wrestling, winning three National Wrestling Alliance-Hollywood Championships and a dozen NWA-Northwest Championships that included five Heavyweight and seven Tag Team titles. All the while, he carved out a successful niche as a commentator in the sport. Beginning in 1968 and for the next two decades, he appeared in 18 Hollywood films, including the role as the Mean Machine Shop Steward in *The Longest Yard.*

#22 Donnie Hixon remembers *"I remember him saying he was born in Canada, played in the Canadian professional football league for a short time before becoming a professional wrestler. He was a rugged, physical looking man whose appearance gave you the looks of one who would do very well in a bar or street fight! The same expectations you would have of actor John Wayne! In the* Superman *movie he played the role of Rocky, the truck driver, which was a good choice by the casting people! Pepper was a very humble and congenial person to be around!"*

Lucile Nelson, *Receptionist*

The soon to be retired receptionist of 26 years at Reidsville prison, Lucile Nelson, played herself in *The Longest Yard.* Some 250 inmates, roughly 10 percent of the prison population, attended the production's first audition. - "Hollywood Goes Behind the Walls at Reidsville," Henry Woodhead, *The Atlanta Journal and Constitution Magazine,* November 25, 1973

James Hooks Nicholson (Reynolds), *Ice Man*

Burt Reynolds' adopted brother, James Hooks Reynolds went by James "Jimmy" Hooks Nicholson at the time *The Longest Yard* was produced. He appeared as a Guards team member in the movie, the first of four acting credits he would earn in Hollywood. James Hooks Reynolds also appeared in *The Presidio* (1988), in two episodes of his brother's *B.L. Stryker* television series (1989-1990), and *Heaven's Prisoners* (1996). Like Burt had been, Jimmy was a stunt man. According to online accounts he also coached football and baseball at Forest Hill Community High School in the West Palm Beach area.

Six months after Burt died at age 83 of cardiac arrest, James Hooks Reynolds died of the same affliction.

#22 Donnie Hixon remembers *"Man, did Jimmy ever receive blessings from the good Lord at 12 years old when he came to live with Mr. and Mrs. Reynolds, who were great parents! Plus he became Burt's adopted brother later. You got to figure when Burt started making his run to stardom, being Burt's adopted brother got him a lot of attention going forward... Jim was an extremely nice guy, and a pleasure to be around! You could tell he really looked up to Burt, who was obviously his hero.*

"The Longest Yard *movie credits show his last name as Nicholson, and that's what his last name was when I met him during the movie. Once while having a conversation with him I remember him saying he was a high school football coach. Many years later after the movie I heard he had changed his last name to Reynolds. He said he grew up with Burt, and I remember him telling me the Reynolds family took care of him at an early age, and what fine people they were. He did share a few stories about Burt and family, surprisingly about what a good football player Burt was, and all the girl attention he got in high school."*

Ray Nitschke

Raymond Ernest "Ray" Nitschke was born near Chicago in 1936 — the same year that Burt Reynolds was born in Lansing, Michigan. Like Reynolds, Nitschke went to the top of his chosen profession. A high school standout, Nitschke dreamed of playing quarterback at Illinois. The youngest of three sons, Nitschke was raised by two older brothers after his parents died, his father in a car accident when he was a young boy, and his mother of a blood clot when he was in his early teens.

Without parental guidance, Ray proved an unruly child, with poor grades in school. Academic ineligibility kept him on the sidelines his sophomore year at Proviso High School in Maywood, Illinois. "I grew up belting the other kids in the neighborhood, Nitschke once recalled, "I felt I was somebody who didn't have anything and I took it out on anybody." When Nitschke returned as a junior, he proved a standout at quarterback, and at safety on defense.

He also proved a force in baseball as a pitcher and outfielder. That presented Nitschke with a major decision when the St. Louis Browns offered him a signing bonus to play professionally. On the advice of high school coach Andy Pupils, Ray was steered to Illinois on a football scholarship, where he'd be one step closer to his ultimate dream of quarterbacking the team to the Rose Bowl.

Green Bay Packers Hall of Fame quarterback Bart Starr, was once quoted as saying about Nitschke, "...he was strong enough to throw a ball 100 yards at time, and 80 yards like it was nothing." During filming of *The Longest Yard*, Burt Reynolds' stunt double, #22 Donnie Hixon, recalled, "While we were on a film break someone challenged him on that. I and others saw him throw it 80 yards... On another day, he threw one 87 yards!"

Old habits die hard and the edgy Nitschke continued his self destructive ways at Champaign-Urbana. According to writer Martin Hendrix in a 2009 article, "The Face of a Smashmouth Approach," Nitschke fought and drank off the field, and his grades in the classroom were nothing to write home about. During his sophomore year, 1955, Nitschke was given the choice of starting at fullback or being the Illini's backup at quarterback by Illinois head coach Ray Eliot. He was at a crossroads and in his autobiography, *Mean on Sunday*, the dejected Nitschke later confessed, "I sat there in his office and cried."

If he didn't shed a tear in the Illini's Big Ten opener his junior year, he had multiple reasons to do so. At a time when football helmets with face masks were a novelty, the rough and tumble Nitschke would not be caught in one during his college career. If playing without a crossbar was good for Sid Luckman and Bronco Nagurski, the Chicago Bears players he idolized in his youth, then it would be good enough for Nitschke too. Fast forward to October 13, 1956.

On the opening kickoff of Illinois' Big Ten opener at home to 5th ranked Ohio State, Nitschke was rocked by an opposing helmet, a blow that cost him two teeth, as two others among the front four danced in their sockets, held only by threads. His mouth packed with cotton, Nitschke played on, and spat blood throughout the game. Adding insult to injury, the Illini lost to the Buckeyes 26-6 and Nitschke came away from the experience with a gap toothed smile that would become his trademark.

His mouth was fitted with a front plate of false teeth to accommodate the gap. According to writer George Plimpton, Nitschke, upon meeting someone who had gone to Ohio State, would pull the plate from his mouth, and proceed to flash a wide smile as he related, "This is what your school did to me."

At 6'3" and 235 pounds, Nitschke was as hard-nosed a player as existed, yet nimble for a man his size. In addition, he possessed a workman's ethic to play hard until the whistle sounded; that is, if he happened to hear one at all. That caught the attention of legendary NFL coach Paul Brown, who believed him to be the unequal of any middle linebacker in the college game. And while Nitschke yearned to play for the hometown Bears professionally, he was chosen in the third round of the NFL Draft on December 2, 1957, by their bitter rivals, the Green Bay Packers.

In the first four rounds of that draft, the Packers picked three future Hall of Famers, Jim Taylor in the second, Nitschke, with their second of two third round choices, and Jerry Kramer in the fourth. All-Pro

Linebacker Dan Currier was picked third overall in the draft. It proved one of the best drafts for any team in NFL history.

According to *Milwaukee Sentinel* writer, Bud Lea, "the Packers 'took a chance' on the unruly Nitschke... They didn't know how to deal with him until Vince Lombardi harnessed Nischke's boundless aggression and anger into the best middle linebacker who ever played the game." In his "Packer Plus" column shortly after Nitschke's death, Lea revealed that "it was characteristic of Lombardi that he went out of his way to treat Nitschke harshly. He really did a job on him." Lombardi was the one man who could reach inside and push just the right buttons with Nitschke. In *Run to Daylight,* Lombardi wrote, "He (Nitschke) can take it. He is a big, tough, belligerent guy with heart as big as all outdoors. You don't improve him, he improves himself."

In his book, *Distant Replay*, Jerry Kramer wrote, "Sometimes I thought of Ray as more of an opponent than a teammate, he inflicted so much damage in practice." He and Jimmy (Taylor), just didn't know what it was like to brother-in-law, to ease up. Former teammate Forrest Gregg also recalled, "Ray was a 100-percenter — a guy that never slacked off. Whether it was a practice or a game, the first play or the last or a close game or a blowout. That's just the kind of player he was." Nitschke once said, "I came to play. I came to practice, too."

His first season with the Packers, Nitschke sported the #33 jersey during a dismal 1-10-1 record. With seven future Hall of Famers and four other Pro-Bowlers on its roster, the 1958 team had talent, but lacked direction. The following year, in Vince Lombardi's first season as head coach, Nitschke was handed the #66 jersey, which he wore the next 14 seasons. The number was twice his previous jersey number, and from that point on the Packers were more than doubly good, winning seven games in 1959 and eight more in 1960. With Lombardi at the controls, the Packers transformed into a dynasty and by 1961 rolled to the first of five NFL Championships in seven seasons.

On Thursday, September 1, 1960, in his third season, Nitschke nearly lost his life during a morning practice session. As a threatening storm with high winds converged on Green Bay, the team huddled between practices at their fields on Oneida Street. It had just started raining and "it looked like it would rain pretty hard," said Nitschke. For a player with a balding head the raindrops proved a bit more annoying, so he put his helmet back on, just as a strong gust of wind kicked up.

The squall knocked a 15-foot, 1,000-pound photographer's tower down on top of Nitschke. According to the account in the next day's Milwaukee Sentinel, "a bolt holding the steel piping together went completely through Nitschke's helmet and stopped just short of his skull... The hole was about four inches above the left temple." While Lombardi rushed to check on the situation, when he found out it was Nitschke under the pile, he reportedly said, "He'll be fine. Get back to work!" Nitschke, too, was apparently unfazed by the incident, and "just got up and continued to practice..." with a new helmet. The helmet that sustained the hole and saved Nitschke's life is now showcased in the Packers Hall of Fame.

In June, 1961, the summer following the hole in the helmet incident, Nitschke married Jackie Forchette. Her calming presence had a profound effect on Ray, who stopped drinking. On the football field, #66 remained the dominant force in the middle of the Packers defense throughout their glory years of the 1960's. In the 1962 NFL Championship game against the New York Giants, a crowd of just under 65,000 huddled in the bitter cold on December 30 at Yankee Stadium. Television crews stoked bonfires to thaw out their cameras. Nitschke played as if he hardly noticed the weather, and corralled two fumbles to go along with a deflected pass turned interception, to earn the game's MVP award in a 16-7 Packers victory.

In the AFL-NFL World Championship Game in January 1967, which concluded the 1966 season and retroactively became Super Bowl I, Nitschke recorded six tackles and a sack in Green Bay's 35-10 victory over Kansas City. The following season of 1967 proved another banner year for the Packers, but not before a date with the Dallas Cowboys in the Ice Bowl Game. Teams were aware of extremely cold weather headed towards Green Bay, but expected the deep freeze to hit the night after the game. Forecasters were a day off. The two teams got their final practices in for the game in balmy 35 degree heat on a perfect field on Saturday, December 30. Temperatures overnight plunged to -21 degrees in Green Bay and players woke up to a new world order the following morning.

"Thirteen degrees below zero," lamented Cowboys' end Frank Clarke. "Oh, God! We weren't prepared for that." Running back Don Perkins thought the hotel operator was kidding when informed of the frigid temperature. "Then I opened the blinds, saw the ice caked on the windows..." Sportswriter Dick Schaap observed the -13 temperature atop a bank marquee and commented, "Look, it's broken" to his wife. The NFL Championship on New Year's Eve remains the coldest game in league history.

At kickoff for the historic Cowboys-Packers game, the temperature stood at -13 degrees, with a wind chill that registered -36 degrees. It got colder as the game progressed, but mattered little to Packer nation, nearly 52,000 of whom packed Lambeau Field that New Year's Eve day. In a scene reminiscent of the tongue to the flag pole scene in *A Christmas Story,* (still 15 years in the future), official Norm Schachter's metal whistle stuck to his lips on the opening kickoff.

When he pulled it from his mouth, the skin on his lips came with it, and blood instantly froze in place. Officials ditched the whistles and were forced instead to verbally shout the end of plays that day.

Earlier that year, Lambeau Field was fitted with an intricate web of 14 miles of underground heating cables, at a cost of eighty-thousand dollars, courtesy General Electric. If ever there was a time to have a sub-surface heating system in place, it would have been that last day of December, 1967. And if only such a setup could be counted on when needed most. After all, the heater operated nicely when tested the day prior to the big game — when temps were 50 degrees warmer. When the blast of arctic air rolled over Green Bay by surprise the night prior to the game, "Murphy's Law — *anything that can go wrong, will go wrong"* was set in motion.

The perfect storm was only compounded by the malfunctioning heating system at Lambeau Field, which begged to be noticed. When groundskeepers finally peeled back the tarp the following day, to their horror, an accumulation of moisture underneath the cover began to freeze in place. In theory, it would not have been a problem if the newly installed 1,700-kilowatt heating system had worked as planned. *If it just hadn't been so darned cold!* By gametime, Lambeau Field was literally a "Frozen Tundra."

Playing in such adverse conditions can place even the toughest of competitors, including Ray Nitschke, under extreme duress. Cowboys end Frank Clarke later recalled the Ice Bowl encounter he had with Ray Nitschke. As he headed back to the huddle after a play, Clarke said, "I got about two feet away from Ray Nitschke, and he turned, and he started screaming at me, *'Get away from me you son of a bitch. I'll break your f****** neck.'* And I looked and he had white froth in the corners of his mouth, and I could see this glare through his face mask..." The Ice Bowl would prove to be the final game in Clarke's 11-year career, the final eight of those with Dallas.

Though Green Bay took an early 14-0 lead on a pair of Bart Starr to Boyd Dowler touchdown passes, the Cowboys roared back for a 17-14 lead as time wound down. The Packers would need to mount a long final drive in an effort to tie, or win the game outright. "The thing I vividly recall," Packers fullback Chuck Mercein later said, "the offense is running on the field and the punt return team is coming off and Ray Nitschke was on the field, screaming at the offense, *'Don't let me down! Don't let me down!'* He was an intimidating figure," Mercein continued. "He had no teeth, snot was coming out of his nose, there was blood and mud on his uniform." As the sight of Nitschke rattled around in his psyche, Mercein, the Milwaukee native, led a charge that accounted for 34 yards of "The Drive," exactly half of the 68 yards the Packers would need.

On third and goal with 16 seconds remaining, the Packers stood at the one-yard line. Quarterback Bart Starr called timeout and proposed a play to coach Vince Lombardi, who simply responded, *"Then run it, and let's get the hell out of here."* It was -18 degrees. So cold that even on television everything seemed in slow motion, too frigid to move. "...I get cold thinking about it" Bart Starr recalled 20 years later. "Before the last play, despite all the noise, it was like being in a vacuum. It was eerily quiet. All I could hear was breathing. All I could see was steam."

The play was designed for Jerry Kramer, and center Ken Bowman to double-team Cowboys tackle, Jethro Pugh, just enough to create an opening, one that could not be found on two previous plays. With frostbite on his fingers, Starr took the snap, but instead of handing the ball to fullback Mercein as the play called for, he surprised his own teammates with what happened next. *"Starr begins the count. Takes the snap... He's got the quarterback sneak and he's in for the touchdown and the Packers are out in front! 20-17! And 13 seconds showing on the clock and the Green Bay Packers are going to be... World Champions, NFL Champions, for the third straight year!"* - Packers radio announcer, Ted Moore

Nitschke author Edward Gruver described the scene in the Packers locker room that followed, in which players, physically exhausted and emotionally drained, openly wept. Even Nitschke discovered his own limitations. Ever the tough guy, he had declined what little warmth the sideline heaters provided during the game. Looking back, Nitschke recalled, "I played pro football 15 years and that was the greatest game I ever played in... Because of the emotion of the game, I was numb all over. I never even thought about my feet. But a couple of hours after the game, we were partying and all my toes blistered off. I couldn't keep my shoes on. I had the flu for a week after the game and lost 10 pounds. But it was worth it all to win like we did that day." Two weeks later, the Packers won Super Bowl II against the Oakland Raiders, 33-14, in Vince Lombardi's final game as head coach in Green Bay.

In a career that spanned 15 seasons, all with Green Bay, Nitschke pounded opposing offenses, intercepted 25 passes, recovered 23 fumbles, and was named All-Pro seven times. He was also named to the NFL's 50- and 75-year Anniversary teams. Nitschke played the game with wild abandon, an ultra-aggressive style that made him a feared opponent throughout the league and a fan favorite in Green Bay. Off the field, Nitschke was a gentleman with a trademark smile, known for having a warm heart for charitable causes, which endeared him even more to the community. Ray and Jackie Nitschke adopted three children and owned a winter home in Naples, Florida, just across the state from Burt Reynolds' home in Jupiter.

During the 1973 preseason, Nitschke was one of three middle linebackers on the roster, and at age 36, the oldest of the Packers. Someone had to go, and #66's number was up. On Tuesday morning, August 28, 1973, Nitschke strode into the Packers admin building at Lambeau Field to face the media alone. Fifteen seasons had come down to 15 minutes. Fighting back tears, Nitschke swallowed hard and announced the inevitable. "I have no complaints and no hard feelings. I'm just glad to have been a Packer." Four years removed from being named to the NFL's All-Pro team, an emotional Nitschke proclaimed, "The only regret I have is that I can't turn the clock back to 1958 and become a Packer all over again."

Then he uttered the words that must have been music to the ears of producers for *The Longest Yard*, "I've taken real good care of myself, and I still have the desire to perform," Nitschke said. "It hasn't been proven that I can't play, but retirement has been in the back of my mind and this is the time for it." It wasn't long before Nitschke was back in uniform, in front of film crews at Reidsville State Prison in south Georgia. The newly retired Nitschke still had game, and proved a memorable addition to *The Longest Yard*, in the character of Guard Bogdanski.

For two months that autumn, Nitschke did what he had always done – play football with unbridled passion, his gap-toothed smile as wide as it had ever been. For Burt Reynolds' stand-in double, #22 Donnie Hixon, that translated into five weeks of punishing hits from the NFL Hall of Famer. Whatever pent up aggression Nitschke carried away as he left the Packers, he took out in therapy sessions on the football field in Georgia as he transitioned to real life. Nitschke was back in the spotlight, able to conclude his notable career with yet another football game in a memorable football movie. Nitschke's therapy proved a major headache for #22 Donnie Hixon, who remains slim and fit at age 78, and sports a mangled ring finger courtesy of his days fending off Nitschke. Hixon also tweaked his right leg during filming. The knee bothered him more and more over the next several years until Hixon had it operated on to repair a torn meniscus. Still, despite the lumps he took during those nine weeks in 1973, Hixon was honored to have taken part in the production. He had measured his game against some of the best to have put on a uniform and stood up to the test.

In 1978, Nitschke was named to the Pro Football Hall of Fame, and five years later the Packers retired his #66 jersey. Ray Nitschke died March 8, 1998, in Venice, Florida, at age 61, the same number he wore on his jersey in *The Longest Yard.* When the Old Main Street Bridge that traversed the Fox River in Green Bay was replaced in 1998, the year Nitschke died, the new structure across the waterway was named Ray Nitschke Memorial Bridge. The Packers' state-of-the-art Ray Nitschke Field, an outdoor practice facility, debuted in 2009.

#22 Donnie Hixon remembers *"When I got out of the Marines, I bought a color TV and started watching football games and became a Green Bay Packer and Coach Lombardi fan. When there was an opportunity, I talked with Ray about Lombardi, the team, and the games, and learned a lot about Lombardi's method of coaching, and just football in general. Ray told me he always played with bad intentions! He said he loved making contact, that his goal was to deliver pain and send a strong message to those he tackled, 'Don't come my way again!'"*

Ray Ogden, *Schmidt (Mean Machine)*

Ogden grew up in Jesup, Georgia, 43 miles south of Reidsville State Prison, where *The Longest Yard* was filmed. He cemented his name in the annals of college football history in 1964 with a 107-yard touchdown return in Alabama's final regular season game against rival Auburn, which the Tide won 21-17. Ogden and quarterback Joe Namath were team captains. Bear Bryant's team finished the regular season unbeaten and were named National Champions in the final AP and UPI polls, prior to the bowl schedule. When Bama was beaten by Texas in the Orange Bowl on New Year's Day, the Football Writers Association awarded unbeaten Arkansas their national title. Ogden was was chosen in the third round of the 1965 NFL Draft and played seven years with four teams, including the St. Louis Cardinals (1965-1966), New Orleans Saints (1967), Atlanta Falcons (1967-1968), and Chicago Bears (1969-1971).

#22 Donnie Hixon remembers *"Ray played tight-end on the Mean Machine in the movie. I remember seeing those great receiving hands of his when throwing the ball to him. Amazing, here I was throwing passes to someone who caught them from the great Joe Namath. I didn't get many stories out of him, as he was on the quiet side, but was very friendly."*

Bernadette Peters, *Miss Toot*

Star of stage and screen for six decades, Peters' professional career began as a nine-year-old in 1958 theatre performance in *Miss Giggle*. Her role as a secretary, Miss Toot, in *The Longest Yard* marked only her second appearance in a film to that point. Peters won her first major award in 1968 with the Theatre World Award for Outstanding Broadway Debut for her performance as Josie Cohan in *George M!* That same year she captured the first of three Drama Desk Awards for Outstanding Actress in a Musical in *Dames at Sea*. In 1981, Peters captured a Golden Globe for her work in *Pennies from Heaven*.

Five years later, Peters proved a double-major award winner with the first of two Tony Awards for Best Actress in a Musical, along with a second Drama Desk Award for her work in *Song and Dance*. In 1999, Peters followed up with a Triple Crown of Theatre Awards, earning her second Tony, third Drama Desk Award, and the Outer Critics Circle Award for Outstanding Actress in a Musical, all for her performance in *Annie Get Your Gun*. The cast recordings of four productions in which Peters has taken part have won Grammys – *Sunday in the Park with George* (1984), *Into The Woods* (1988), *Annie Get Your Gun* (1999), and *Gypsy* (2003).

#22 Donnie Hixon remembers *"I never had any contact with her, but would have loved to have met her. One day I heard a member of the film crew comment on what a beautiful person she was, and what a lot of fun it was filming her part with Burt."*

Sonny Shroyer, *Tannen*

On a drive from Tallahassee, Florida, to Reidsville, Georgia, (site of *The Longest Yard* filming) you will pass through the town of Valdosta, roughly the one-third mark of your journey. All three towns are a big part of Sonny Shroyer's life story. At the same time that Burt Reynolds was a high school football star in West Palm Beach, Florida, Shroyer was a standout in football-crazed Valdosta, where he played on two state championship teams under legendary coach Wright Bazemore. Like Reynolds, Shroyer earned a scholarship to FSU in Tallahassee – and also like Burt, his career was derailed by injury. Though he met Reynolds at FSU, the two were a year apart in school and were more acquaintances than friends.

Fast forward nearly three decades and that's where Reidsville enters the picture for the two football players-turned actors. Ironically, it was the back cover of the 1961 Georgia-Georgia Tech football program where he appeared in football gear that kickstarted Shroyer's career. Aside from his character as Tannen in *The Longest Yard*, Shroyer's list of credits includes two more films with Reynolds, *Gator* (1976), and *Smokey and the Bandit* (1977). Best known from the *Dukes of Hazzard* television series, where he played the role of Deputy Sheriff Enos Strate, Shroyer got back to his football roots when he appeared as legendary Alabama coach Bear Bryant in *Forrest Gump*, (1994).

#22 Donnie Hixon remembers *"Sonny was really a super nice guy. He would sometimes do those silly facial expressions and talk the same way his character, Tannen, did in* The Longest Yard, *and again later down the road as his character in the TV series. That was his niche. He was pretty good at it because he practiced it enough around us all the time. Sometimes some of us would get tired of hearing it. He was the type of person you couldn't get mad at, and wouldn't want to hurt his feelings. You got to give it to the kid from Valdosta, he did well. Sonny was funny and a good person.*

"The last day of filming, the lady in the restaurant by the motels cooked Sonny and some of us peach cobbler pies. She made them for dessert, which we could enjoy after evening meals. I'm talking delicious. I remember eating almost a whole pie on an empty stomach that day, and got sick as a dog – from too much sugar. Today, whenever I eat peach cobbler pie, I think about that day sitting across from Sonny and the others eating that pie. I also remember the good lessons I learned from it. Number one, don't overindulge. Number two, whatever you do, do not eat on an empty stomach. That's where I made the mistake."

Sonny Sixkiller, *The Indian (Mean Machine)*

Born in the Cherokee Nation in Oklahoma, Sixkiller was raised in southern Oregon, where he was a force to be reckoned with in three sports in high school, including football. A second team All-State selection at quarterback earned him a scholarship to the University of Washington, where appropriate of his name, he donned the #6 jersey. With Sixkiller at quarterback, the Huskies turned their program around, taking a 1-9 record the previous season to a formidable 6-4 mark as a sophomore, when he passed for 2,303 yards and 15 touchdowns. Washington went 8-3 in each of Sixkiller's final two seasons in college, after which he played two seasons in the now defunct World Football League. On the roster of the Philadelphia Bell in 1974, Sixkiller ended his career in Honolulu the following year, where he threw for seven touchdowns for the Hawaiians.

In a memorable scene in *The Longest Yard*, after Unger introduces Burt Reynolds' character, Paul Crewe to Sixkiller's persona, The Indian. The exchange went as follows: Crewe: "Heard you played some football." The Indian: "Yeah" Crewe: "Where?" The Indian: "Oklahoma State" Crewe: "Oklahoma State U?" The Indian: "Prison."

John "Pop" Steadman, *Pop (Mean Machine)*

A radio personality for 30 years prior to embarking on a second career in film, Steadman appeared in two other films with Burt Reynolds, *White Lightning* (1973), and *Gator* (1976). Among his character roles in 27 films, Steadman worked in two other Bob Aldrich-directed movies, *Emperor of the North* (1973), and *The Frisco Kid* (1979). His role as Pop in *The Longest Yard* is likely his most memorable. (Steadman was 64 when the movie was filmed in the fall of 1973).

Robert Tessier, *Connie Shokner (Mean Machine)*

Like Eddie Albert, Tessier earned medals serving in the military. During the Korean War, Tessier was a paratrooper who won a Silver Star to go along with a Purple Heart for injuries sustained in combat. After the war, the motorcycle stunt rider turned actor Tessier made a career out of playing badass characters in television and movie roles. His memorable performance as Connie Shokner, the karate-expert convict on The Mean Machine in *The Longest Yard* only helped cement that notion. Tessier played a role familiar to him, as a biker, in another film starring Burt Reynolds, *The Cannonball Run* (1981). Robert "Bob" Tessier passed away in 1990 at age 56.

#22 Donnie Hixon remembers *"He looked the part! He didn't have to act, just be himself!...In talking with him I remember he was 39 years old, born the same year my older brother Richard who got killed at age 17. He has been in many film and television shows before, and since* The Longest Yard. *With that shaved head and muscular physique, he was a natural for film roles in need of an actor that could depict a gang leader, thug, or biker (he was a circus stunt motorcycle performer).*

"It seemed Bob didn't spend much time playing football growing up. In the scene where he broke Dick Kiel's (Samson's) nose in a rehearsed football scene, Tessier was having trouble understanding the football stance and positions. Joe Kapp (Walking Boss) lost his patience trying to explain to him how to do it right. Joe was finding it hard to get across to an actor in such a short time, one who had obviously never played the game before. Kapp was really losing it, and started yelling and giving Bob hell while using curse words. It was then that Bob went into his karate attack stance and dared Joe to 'bring it.' Joe stayed away from him about eight feet and circled him several times, trying to decide if he should fight with Tessier or not. Just about the time Joe was ready to go at him, the associate director and one of the film crew broke things up just in time! A fight between Bob, a karate expert, and a big badass like Joe Kapp would have been a sight to see. Who would I have picked to win? Joe survived hits in the NFL that came from some of the toughest, meanest men on the planet whose intentions were very bad. The name of the game in those days was kill the quarterback! Back when he played, they didn't

have all those rules to protect the quarterback like they do today. With that in mind, I would have had to put my money on Joe, who had been battle-tested many times in the NFL. The fight would have been a good one!"

Charles Tyner, *Unger*

Tyner began his career in theatre and in 1959 appeared alongside Paul Newman on Broadway in *Sweet Bird of Youth*. Impressed with Tyner's acting skills, Newman selected him for the role of the ultra-cruel prison guard Boss Higgins in *Cool Hand Luke* (1967). Seven years later, Tyner was cast in an equally impressive role in yet another prison movie, this time as Unger, the sniveling snitch who murders Caretaker in *The Longest Yard*. Tyner's memorable line in *The Longest Yard* is "How do ya like them apples, Superstar?" Tyner died in November, 2017 at the age of 92.

Ernie "Wheels" Wheelwright, *Spooner (Mean Machine)*

Wheelwright was three years removed from a seven-year NFL career when he played Spooner in *The Longest Yard*. As a professional football player, Wheelright played for the Giants (1964-1965), Falcons (1966-1967), and Saints (1967-1970). The versatile Wheelwright compiled a 3.7 yard rushing average and 9 touchdowns in his career, along with 7 TD receptions and an average of 9.8 yards per catch. Aside from *The Longest Yard*, Wheelwright also appeared in role of Rosie in *Trackdown* (1976), as Bossman Jones in Muhammed Ali's *The Greatest* (1977), and as a coach in *Wildcats* (1986).

#22 Donnie Hixon remembers *"Wheelwright told me he served in the U.S. Army in the 101st Airborne Division (Screaming Eagles) and that he played college football at Southern Illinois University... He was a 6'3" 240 pound fullback, running the football and catching the ball in* *the NFL. His weight (for* The Longest Yard*) had reached up to 275 pounds. He was huge! He reported looking in great shape and was the left offensive tackle on the Mean Machine. I remember throwing him a tackle eligible pass, and watching him reach for and grab the ball with those big hands, then run toward the goal line like a runaway Mack truck. Ernie was very intelligent and a cool person."*

Other Cast and Crew

Alan P. Horowitz, *Associate Producer;* Tracy Keenan Wynn, *Screenwriter;* Gerald Michael Atkins, *Football Player;* Joe Dorsey, *Bartender;* J. Don Ferguson, *Referee;* Lance Fuller, *Secondary Role;* Chuck Hayward, *Trooper;* Stan Kanavage, *"Charlie Blue Eyes;"* Harold Morris, *Minor Role;* Jack Rockwell, *Trainer;* Buddy Satcher, *Guard;* Wilson Warren, *"Buttercup;"* Dino Washington, *"Mason;"* Philip Wende, *Guard;* Alfie Wise, *Trooper*

Guards vs. Prisoners II

Two years after *The Longest Yard* wrapped up at Reidsville State Prison, in 1975, a team comprised of Georgia State Troopers and Prison Guards faced off against a group of inmates. The occasion was a benefit football game, during Christmas season, on the same field that Burt Reynolds helped make famous. According to *The New York Times*, some 1,500 fans were in attendance.

Local residents stood on one side of the field, and prisoners watched from a vantage point on the other side of the field. The newspaper account reported that inmates shouted, among other things, "Stick it to the police!" Warden Joe Hopper and his staff took it all in good stride. Like in the 1974 release of *The Longest Yard*, the prisoners won again. Unlike in the Burt Reynolds movie, this time it was a rout, 51-0.

The contest was played just prior to Christmas to raise money for 7-year-old Bobby Boyles, whose mom worked at the prison and whose dad was a highway patrolman. The youngster had begun receiving cobalt treatments late that year to combat a "large tumor at the stem of the child's brain." The inmates' concern for the young boy caused Bobby's mom to remark, in keeping with the holiday season, "This just shows you there is some good in everybody, I suppose."

Special Thanks

To Bill Baab, my longtime friend, editor extraordinaire and Augusta historian. Baab began his career with *The Augusta Chronicle* in 1955 and nearly 65 years later, continues to produce the newspaper's Fishing Page. This is the third book that Baab has edited for this author. Other titles include *Augusta and Aiken in Golf's Golden Age* (2002), and *The Augusta National Golf Club; Alister MacKenzie's Masterpiece* (2005).

To Jeff Hadden and the staff at Phoenix Commercial Printing for their ongoing friendship, support and dedication to excellence, and to Cathleen Wedding and Robin Raymond for their expertise in layout and creative. Jeff and the Phoenix Family have built one of the most amazing businesses in the world in downtown Augusta.

To Beverly Hixon, for her aid in shoring up the endless trail of details – proofing, praying, pushing, negotiating, marketing, accounting and all those things that need to be done today to keep a book project on track.

Special thanks to Warden Marty Allen, the staff at Reidsville State Prison and the Georgia Department of Corrections in the making of this book. Nearly a half-century after its production, the 1974 release of *The Longest Yard* remains a source of pride at the prison and in surrounding communities that support its cause.

This book further stands as a lasting memorial to Dan Harrison, *slain in the line of duty, July 23, 1978,* while serving at Reidsville State Prison, and as a gesture of appreciation to all those who stand guard at prison facilities throughout the nation.

Photography Credits

Donnie Hixon Collection of Hixon family photos

Donnie Hixon Collection, photos taken by Tom Goforth at Reidsville State Prison in the fall of 1973.

Stan Byrdy Collection, photos taken on February 1, 2018, Courtesy Reidsville State Prison

Paramount Pictures, promotional photos, *The Longest Yard*

Bibliography

Memoirs of Donnie Hixon
My Life, Burt Reynolds Autobiography, 1994, Hyperion, New York
"Remembering Reidsville... and Burt Reynolds," Stan Byrdy, *Columbia County Magazine,* September, 2018
"Man Hangs Self In Police Lockup," *The Augusta Chronicle,* October 21, 1949
The Academy of Richmond County, 2015-16 Hall of Fame inductees
All-Time Georgia Football Lettermen, *georgiadogs.com*
All-Time Georgia Basketball Lettermen, *georgiadogs.com*
All-Time Georgia Baseball Lettermen, *georgiadogs.com*
Pat Dye, *Wikipedia*
Nat Dye, *Wikipedia*
All-Time Georgia Football Lettermen
Canadian Football League, *justsportsstats.com*
The Three Faces of Eve, Wikipedia
Hervey M. Cleckley, *Wikipedia*
Corbett M. Thigpen, *Wikipedia*
"Luzerne County Sports Hall of Fame, 1989 Inductee, Frances Lovecchio," *luzernecountysportshalloffame.com*
"The day the old Bermudiana died,'"Jessie Moniz, *The Royal Gazette,* May 17, 2012
"The Augusta Riots: 45 Years Later," Stacey Eidson, *Metro Spirit,* May 2, 2015
"3 Dead in Augusta Riots," *The Augusta Chronicle,* May 12, 1970
"Someone has to talk to the kids," Jeff Smoller, *The Augusta Chronicle,* May 13, 1970
"Man Hangs Self In Police Lockup," *The Augusta Chronicle,* October 20, 1949
"Musketeers faced tragedy in title run," "The Way We Were," Bill Kirby, *The Augusta Chronicle* Monday, April 29, 2019
Cosmopolitan magazine, April, 1972
"McAlester Prison Riot," *The Encyclopedia of Oklahoma History and Culture,* Oklahoma Historical Society
"Three Days of Mayhem: the McAlester Riot," Shaun Hittle, *oklahomawatch.org,* July 25, 2013
"Remembering Reidsville...and Burt Reynolds," Stan Byrdy, *Columbia County Magazine,* October, 2018
"Hollywood Goes Behind the Walls at Reidsville," Henry Woodhead, *The Atlanta Journal and Constitution Magazine,* November 25, 1973
"Four Flee to Sweet, Sweet Freedom," *The Atlanta Constitution,* Tuesday, November 6, 1973
Brother Rat, Wikipedia
Joe Kapp, *Wikipedia*
"The Anatomy of a Miracle," Ron Fimrite, *Sports Illustrated,* September 1, 1983
"Ex-Viking, Film Member Arrested on 4 Charges," *Savannah Morning News,* Sunday, November 4, 1973
"Prisoners Rout Guards - In Game to Help Ill Boy," *The New York Times,* December 22, 1975
"Longest Yard' with local touch," Robert Eubanks, *The Augusta Chronicle,* Sunday, 1974.

The Longest Yard (1974), Wikipedia
The Longest Yard (1974), Quotes, IMDb.com
The Longest Yard (1974), *Movie Script, Springfield! Springfield!, springfieldspringfield.co.uk*
"Augusta's Hixon overcame childhood adversities," Dudley Martin, *The Augusta Chronicle, Augusta Herald,* Sunday Morning, July 12, 1987
"Burt Reynolds' funeral held in West Palm Beach," *The Palm Beach Post, palmbeachpost.com,* September 20, 2018
Telephone interviews with Sharon Moore, Bob Rogers, Gloria Jean Shanks, Benny Cheek, and Don Tyre

BURT REYNOLDS

Burt Reynolds, IMDb
My Life, Burt Reynolds Autobiography, 1994, Hyperion, New York
Wikipedia, Butterfield Township, Michigan
"Sally Field mourns the death of her Smokey and the Bandit co-star...," Ross McDonagh, *Daily Mail,* September 6, 2018
"Roles Burt Reynolds Turned Down, From Bond to Solo," *Variety,* September 6, 2018
"Burt Reynolds turned down these iconic roles...," Jason Guerrasio, *Business Insider,* March 17, 2016
Burton Leon Reynolds, Jr. (1936-2018), Genealogy
Burt Reynolds Bio, *Seminoles.com,* June 17, 2014
"How NC State's football team turned Burt Reynolds into a movie star," Chip Alexander, *The News & Observer,* September 18, 2017
"Talking with Burt Reynolds," Chris Nashawaty, EW.com, April 25, 2005
"The Athletic Boyhood of Actor Burt Reynolds," Marc Myers interview, *The Wall Street Journal,* January 19, 2016
"Dog Years' Star Burt Reynolds Dishes on De Niro, Brando, Eastwood and 'Star Wars," Thelma Adams, *Observer,* April 26, 2017
"Burt Reynolds Turned Down "Boogie Nights" 7 Times," *CONAN on TBS,* March 20, 2018
"Memories of *The Longest Yard,*" #22 Donnie Hixon
"The Dawning of Evening Shade...," David Wallace, *LA Times,* February 17, 1991
"The Hell-Raising, Girl-Chasing Boyhood Years of Burt Reynolds," Gerry Hunt, *National Enquirer,* circa 1979
Memoirs of Donnie Hixon

RAY NITSCHKE

Ray Nitschke, *Wikipedia*
1962 NFL Championship Game, *Wikipedia*
1967 NFL Championship Game, *Wikipedia*
Ray Nitschke Memorial Bridge, *Wikipedia*
Ray Nitschke Stats, *Pro-Football-Reference.com*
History of the National Football League Championship, *Wikipedia*
"The Ice Bowl," *Pro Football Hall of Fame Official Site*
"Ice Bowl Remembered..." *The Dallas Morning News,* December 31, 1987
"Ice Bowl II? Packers, Cowboys who played in original know nothing can compare," Sam Gardner, *foxsports.com,* January 7, 2015
"Top 10 Things You Didn't Know About the Green Bay Packers," Frances

Romero, THE GREEN AND GOLD, The Frozen Tundra, *TIME, content.time.com,* February 4, 2011
"Plain and simple: Ray Nitschke was the Packers," Bud Lea, *Milwaukee Journal Sentinel,* April 1, 1998
Ray Nitschke, The Official Website of Ray Nitschke, Nitschke quote, *cmgww.com,* CMG Worldwide
"The face of a smashmouth approach," Martin Hendricks, *jsonline.com, The Milwaukee Journal Sentinal,* February 24, 2009
"He Was Football," Neil Hayes, *pressreader.com, Chicago Sun-Times,* October 19, 2008
"The Lives They Lived: Ray Nitschke; Hard Man In the Middle," George Plimpton, *The New York Times Magazine,* January 3, 1999
"The 1966 Green Bay Packers: Profiles of Vince Lombardi's Super Bowl I Champions," Edited by George Bozeka, *Professional Football Researchers Association*
Mean on Sunday, The Autobiograhy of Ray Nitschke, Ray Nitschke and Robert W. Wells, Doubleday, 1973
Nitschke, The Ray Nitscke Story, Edward Gruver, Taylor Trade Publishing, 2002
"Ray of Hope Dies for Old Pro Nitschke," Bud Lea, *The Milwaukee Sentinel,* August 29, 1973
"Green Bay veteran announces retirement," Associated Press, *The Spokesman-Review* (Seattle), Wednesday, August 29, 1973
"Pack Hall of Famer Nischke dies at 61," *New York Times News Service,* March 9, 1998
"Linebacker stricken by heart attack," *The Baltimore Sun,* March 9, 1998
"Ray Nitschke, 61, Linebacker During Packers' Glory Years," Richard Goldstein, *New York Times,* March 9, 1998
Memoirs of Donnie Hixon
"Murphy's Law," *Wikipedia*

ROBERT ALDRICH, *DIRECTOR*

"All Time Letter Winners," *virginiasports.com*
"Iconoclasts/Robert Aldrich: Going For Broke," David Thompson, *DGA Quarterly,* Spring, 2010
Robert Aldrich, *Wikipedia*
The Longest Yard (1974) Full Cast & Crew, IMDb
My Life, Burt Reynolds Autobiography, 1994, Hyperion, New York
Memoirs of Donnie Hixon

ALBERT S. RUDDY, *PRODUCER*

"Sports Guy's Top Sports Stories," Simmons, Bill, *ESPN.com*
The Longest Yard (1974) Full Cast & Crew, IMDb
Al Ruddy, IMDb
Albert S. Ruddy, *Wikipedia*

EDDIE ALBERT, *WARDEN HAZEN*

Memoirs of Donnie Hixon
"Eddie Albert, Character Actor, Dies at 99," Margalit Fox, *New York Times,* May 28, 2005
Eddie Albert, *Wikipedia*

The Longest Yard (1974) Full Cast & Crew, IMDb

PERVIS ATKINS, *MAWABE (MEAN MACHINE)*

Memoirs of Donnie Hixon

Pervis Atkins, *Wikipedia*

List of NCAA Major College Football Yearly Rushing Leaders, *Wikipedia*

Pervis Atkins, *College Football at Sports-Reference.com*

1959 Rushing Stats, *College Football at Sports-Reference.com*

The Longest Yard (1974) Full Cast & Crew, IMDb

AUGUSTA EAGLES

Memoirs of Donnie Hixon

"Longest Yard' with local touch," Robert Eubanks, *The Augusta Chronicle,* Sunday, 1974

TONY CACCIOTTI, *ROTKA (MEAN MACHINE)*

Tony Cacciotti, *Wikipedia*

The Longest Yard (1974) Full Cast & Crew, IMDb

HARRY CAESAR, *GRANVILLE (MEAN MACHINE)*

Harry Caesar, IMDb

The Longest Yard (1974 film), *Wikiquote*

The Longest Yard (1974) Full Cast & Crew, IMDb

Memoirs of Donnie Hixon

CHEERLEADERS

Memoirs of Donnie Hixon

MICHAEL CONRAD, *NATE SCARBORO (MEAN MACHINE)*

Memoirs of Donnie Hixon

Michael Conrad, *Wikipedia*

Michael Conrad: Nate Scarboro, *The Longest Yard,* IMBd

ANITRA FORD, *MELISSA*

Anitra Ford, *Wikipedia*

Anitra Ford Biography, IMDb

The Longest Yard (1974) Full Cast & Crew, IMBd

MICHAEL FOX, *ANNNOUNCER*

The Longest Yard (1974) Full Cast & Crew, IMDb

JAMES HAMPTON, *CARETAKER (MEAN MACHINE)*

James Hampton, *Wikipedia*

James Hampton: Caretaker, *The Longest Yard,* imdb.com

The Longest Yard (1974) Full Cast & Crew, IMDb

MIKE HENRY, *RASSMEUSEN (GUARDS)*

Memoirs of Donnie Hixon

Mike Henry, *Wikipedia*

The Longest Yard (1974) Full Cast & Crew, IMDb

JOE KAPP, *WALKING BOSS*

BC Lions Retired Numbers, BC.com

Joe Kapp, *Wikipedia*

The Longest Yard (1974) Full Cast & Crew, IMDb

Memoirs of Donnie Hixon

RICHARD "DICK" KIEL, *SAMSON*

"Richard Kiel dies at 74, actor played 'Jaws' in Bond movies," Steve Chawkins, *Los Angeles Times,* September 11, 2014

Richard Kiel, *Wikipedia*
The Longest Yard (1974) Full Cast & Crew, IMDb
Memoirs of Donnie Hixon

ED LAUTER, *CAPTAIN KNAUER*

"Ed Lauter dies at 74; character actor in films and television," Claire Noland, *Los Angeles Times*, October 16, 2013
Ed Lauter, *Wikipedia*
The Longest Yard (1974) Full Cast & Crew, IMDb
Memoirs of Donnie Hixon

MORT MARSHALL, *ASSISTANT WARDEN*

Mort Marshall, List of Movies and TV Shows, *TV Guide*
Mort Marshall, *behindthevoiceactors.com*
The Longest Yard (1974) Full Cast & Crew, IMDb

PEPPER MARTIN, *SHOP STEWARD (MEAN MACHINE)*

Pepper Martin, *Wikipedia*
Pepper Martin, *Cagematch.net*, Titles
The Longest Yard (1974) Full Cast & Crew, IMDb
Memoirs of Donnie Hixon

LUCILE NELSON, *RECEPTIONIST*

"Hollywood Goes Behind the Walls at Reidsville, Henry Woodhead, *The Atlanta Journal and Constitution Magazine*, November 25, 1973

JAMES HOOKS NICHOLSON (REYNOLDS), *ICE MAN*

Memoirs of Donnie Hixon
James Hooks Reynolds, IMDb
James Hooks Reynolds, Linkedin
James Hook Reynolds, *palmbeachhighschool.ning.com*

RAY OGDEN, *SCHMIDT (MEAN MACHINE)*

Memoirs of Donnie Hixon
Ray Ogden, *Wikipedia*
1964 College Football Season, *Wikipedia*
1964 Alabama Crimson Tide Football Team, *Wikipedia*
"Iron Bowl look back: 1964," Mark Edwards, Special to the *Montgomery Advertiser*, November 22, 2016
The Longest Yard (1974) Full Cast & Crew, IMDb

OTHER CAST AND CREW

The Longest Yard (1974) Full Cast & Crew, IMDb

BERNADETTE PETERS, *MISS TOOT*

Bernadette Peters, *Wikipedia*
The Longest Yard (1974) Full Cast & Crew, IMDb
Memoirs of Donnie Hixon

SONNY SHROYER, *TANNEN*

Sonny Shroyer, Biography, IMDb
Sonny Shroyer, *Wikipedia*
The Longest Yard (1974) Full Cast & Crew, IMDb
Memoirs of Donnie Hixon

SONNY SIXKILLER, *THE INDIAN (MEAN MACHINE)*

Sonny Sixkiller, *Wikipedia*

Sonny Sixkiller Statistics, *JustSportsStats.com*
The Longest Yard (1974) Full Cast & Crew, IMDb
Sonny Sixkiller: The Indian, *The Longest Yard, imdb.com*
JOHN "POP" STEADMAN, *POP (MEAN MACHINE)*
John Steadman, *Wikipedia*
The Longest Yard (1974) Full Cast & Crew, IMDb
ROBERT TESSIER, *CONNIE SHOKNER (MEAN MACHINE)*
Robert Tessier, *Wikipedia*
The Longest Yard (1974) Full Cast & Crew, IMDb
Memoirs of Donnie Hixon
CHARLES TYNER, *UNGER*
Charles Tyner, *Wikipedia*
The Longest Yard (1974) Full Cast & Crew, IMDb
ERNIE "WHEELS" WHEELWRIGHT, *SPOONER (MEAN MACHINE)*
Memoirs of Donnie Hixon
Ernie Wheelwright, *Wikipedia*
Ernie Wheelwright Stats, *Pro-Football-Reference.com*
The Longest Yard (1974) Full Cast & Crew, IMDb
Trackdown (1976) Full Cast & Crew, IMDb
The Greatest (1977) Full Cast & Crew, IMBd
Wildcats (1986) Full Cast & Crew, IMDb

Donnie with his mom, Dorothy Lundy Hixon, at his first home on Jenkins Street.

Dorothy Lundy Hixon with sons Gerald and Donnie, age 5.

Donnie's dad, Foster Hixon (L), worked for Georgia Railroad. This is one of only two photos Donnie has of his father, who was beaten by police and died while in custody.

Hixon's older brother Richard was his hero. A star pitcher for the Richmond Academy baseball team, he died after his scooter was hit by a car that ran a stop sign.

Richard Hixon's high school graduation picture. Donnie's oldest brother died just three weeks prior to high school graduation.

1951 Richmond Academy state champion baseball team pitchers. Richard Hixon is shown kneeling bottom left, with Roy Alewine, and Donald "Swifty" Berry. Top row left to right are Kenneth Merry, Jimmy Shead, and Wayne Boose.

Benefit baseball game between Richmond Academy and Boys' Catholic High to raise funds for Richard Hixon's funeral expenses. Over $1,700 was raised, enough for grave markers for Donnie's brother and father, who passed away just 16 months earlier.

Unveiling of grave markers for Richard Hixon and Foster Hixon. Donnie stands alone in front and to the right of his mom, and brother Gerald is on left. The three other students, Bobby Baggott, Nath Hayes, and Tommy Herndon were classmates who raised funds for the markers.

1953 Augusta Biddy League All-Star team included bottom row, left to right: Donnie Hixon, Bonnie Burke, Banks Bowling, and Dunbar Dykes. Top row, left to right: Billy Marshall, Dexter Brooks, Bob Alston, Jack Bearden, Brigham Woodward, and Benny Cheek.

Fat Man's Sanitary Curb Market, where Donnie Hixon worked in the 1950s.

Parris Island Marine graduation picture of Donnie Hixon in 1959. Semper Fi.

Hixon was the starting quarterback on the Marine football team coached by Princeton great Francis Lovecchio.

The USS Chilton, APA 38, Donnie Hixon's home for six months on a tour of the Mediterranean.

Bermuda Marine football trophy presentation to Donnie from Major Hillmer F. DeAtley.

Donnie Hixon, captain of the Bermuda Marine fastpitch softball team. Hixon is standing top center.

Hixon receives three-year good conduct medal in the Marines.

16 Donnie Hixon
QB 180 5'11"

Augusta Eagles quarterback Donnie Hixon in 1971. Two years later he'd play the stunt double for Burt Reynolds in *The Longest Yard.*

Augusta Eagles, 1973. At left, Donnie was the offensive coach, and is shown with Hardy King, Tom Goforth, Calvin Holland, and head coach, Gerald Hixon, Donnie's brother, who played on the same line as football legend Pat Dye at Richmond Academy. This was the same year that Donnie was cast in *The Longest Yard.*

Donnie Hixon at the Augusta College Fashion Show (1977, photo courtesy of Mary Boynton.)

Burt Reynolds autographed picture given to Hixon in 1973 during the filming of *The Longest Yard.*

Burt Reynolds and director Bob Aldrich share ideas during production of *The Longest Yard.*

Donnie Hixon with actor Ed Lauter and former Minnesota Vikings great Joe Kapp in Reidsville, Georgia.

Taking a well deserved break from filming. Paramount Pictures spent $100,00 to have a football field constructed at Reidsville State Prison in south Georgia for production of *The Longest Yard.*

Though he and Burt Reynolds wore #22 jerseys during production, for the Paramount Pictures cast photo Donnie Hixon (pictured upper row, far right) wore the Guards team jersey that he also appeared in during select scenes in the movie. The move further ensured that there would be only one #22 of record.

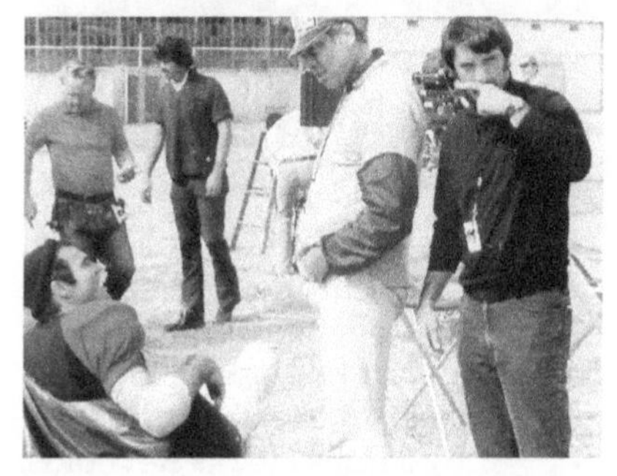

Burt Reynolds with former NFL stars Joe Kapp and Pat Studstill, *The Longest Yard* technical advisor.

Tom Goforth, Burt Reynolds, and Donnie during filming.

Burt Reynolds and Donnie Hixon during production of Paramount Pictures box-office sensation, 1973's *The Longest Yard.*

Eddie Albert and Donnie Hixon in front of the water tower at Reidsville State Prison.

Burt Reynolds, Dr. Gus Carlucci, and actor John "Pop" Steadman, who later played the character of Reynold's dad in the movie *Gator*.

Temperatures in the late fall of '73 dipped near freezing on some mornings in Reidsville, Georgia, as Donnie and Burt Reynolds bundle up from the cold.

Actor Ed Lauter and Jim Nicholson, Burt Reynolds' adopted brother. Named Jimmy Hooks when Burt befriended him as a youngster, in later years he went by James Hooks Reynolds.

Former NFL star Pervis Atkins and Donnie, the other #22. Hixon threw a long touchdown to Atkins' character Muwabe in the movie.

Richard "Dick" Kiel, the 7'4" giant, and Donnie. Kiel played Samson in *The Longest Yard* and later starred as Jaws in two James Bond films.

NFL great Joe Kapp during production — you should have seen the other guy!

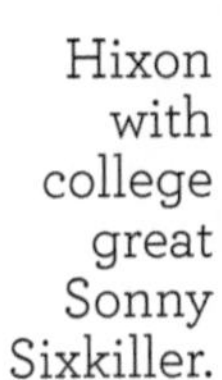

Hixon with college great Sonny Sixkiller.

Donnie and actor Bob Tessier, who played the role of Connie Shockner in *The Longest Yard.*

Burt Reynolds, Augusta Eagles player Tony Reese, and NFL Hall of Famer Ray Nitschke.

Former NFL player Mike Henry on the left starred in three Tarzan movies from 1966-'68. Donnie Hixon shown in the center with NFL great Ray Nitschke on the right.

Burt Reynolds' girlfriend Dinah Shore visits Reidsville State Prison during filming of *The Longest Yard.*

Guards team players: Former NFL standout Mike Henry on the left is shown next to Augusta Eagles player Bobby Meybohm and Ray Nitschke.

Mean Machine team players: George Jones (aka Big George), Steve Wilder (aka J.J), and Wilbur Gillian (aka Big Wilbur). Actor Bob Tessier, who played Connie Shockner in the movie, pulled a prank on the three lineman with a cottonmouth snake during production.

Director Bob Adrich and actor Eddie Albert, who played the warden in *The Longest Yard.*

Actor Bob Tessier portrayed the menacing "Connie Shockner" in *The Longest Yard*. The feared martial arts expert is shown being escorted from "Citrus State Prison."

With former NFL players and semi-pros from the Augusta Eagles taking part, director Bob Aldrich procured authentic action scenes for *The Longest Yard*. Action on the field was fierce as players prepared "to make it real."

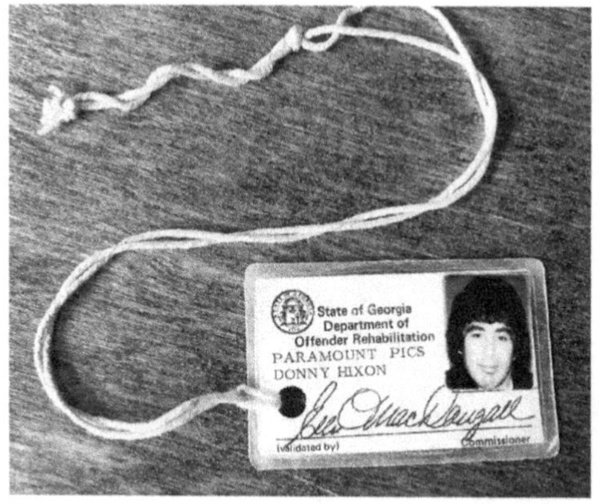

Donnie Hixon was one of 16 members of the Augusta Eagles football team issued ID cards by Paramount Pictures for entry into Reidsville State Prison along with former NFL standouts and Hollywood actors for filming of *The Longest Yard* in the fall of 1973.

Cast and crew prepare to film scenes for *The Longest Yard.*

At 7'4", Dick Kiel as "Samson" stood head and shoulders above the cast and crew at "Citrus State Prison."

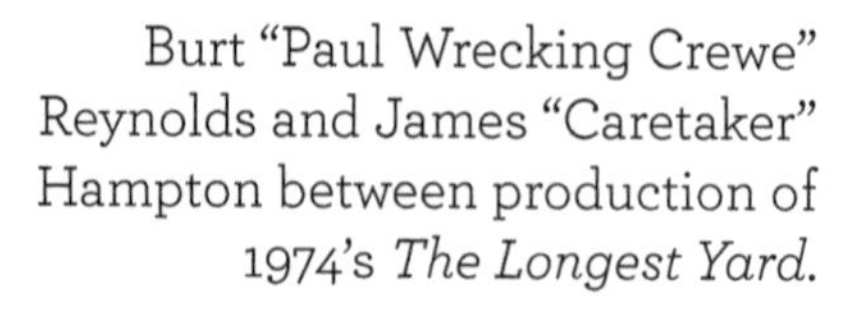

Burt "Paul Wrecking Crewe" Reynolds and James "Caretaker" Hampton between production of 1974's *The Longest Yard.*

Mean Machine running back Joe Jackson, to whom Burt Reynolds gave the nickname "Joe Jack" and an autographed photo.

Burt Reynolds and Donnie's first wife, Patrice Hixon and their son, Travis.

Don Tyre and NFL great Ray Nitschke who had retired from the Green Bay Packers just prior to filming *The Longest Yard.*

South Carolina and NFL star Alex Hawkins and Donnie during the filming of *Gator,* Burt Reynolds' directorial debut, in 1976.

The game changer — wedding day in August 1994 — Donnie and his wife, Beverly Hixon.

Donnie in front of Burt Reynolds' office in Jupiter, Florida, 1993.

Legendary Georgia All-American and University of Auburn head coach Pat Dye and Donnie in Tiger Stadium in 1998. Pat signed the picture to Donnie, "...You beat all the odds."

Warden Marty Allen and Donnie Hixon at Reidsville State Prison, February 1, 2018. It marked Hixon's first visit to the maximum security facility since the filming of *The Longest Yard* in 1973.

Warden Marty Allen proudly displays his Georgia Bulldog chair in his office at Reidsville State Prison in 2018.

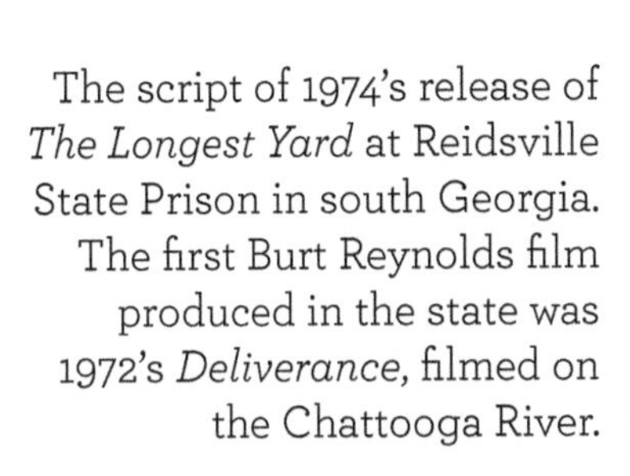

The script of 1974's release of *The Longest Yard* at Reidsville State Prison in south Georgia. The first Burt Reynolds film produced in the state was 1972's *Deliverance,* filmed on the Chattooga River.

Fifth floor window at Reidsville State Prison overlooking the area where a football field was constructed for production of *The Longest Yard* in 1973.

CPSIA information can be obtained
at www.ICGtesting.com
Printed in the USA
LVHW082259161219
640742LV00010B/1231/P

9 781087 815015